D1743973

The Ideal in the West

David A. Beardsley

Ideograph
Media

Copyright © 2012 David A. Beardsley

Graphics are not copyrighted and are believed to be in the public domain.

All rights reserved.

ISBN:1477495185
ISBN-13: 978-1477495186
2nd edition

DEDICATION

To the *Agathon,* in all its names,
and to all its emissaries who have kept those names alive.

Table of Contents

Preface: An overview of the Ideal

Part 1: A History of The Ideal

Chapter I: The Greek Religious Environment................2

The "Establishment" Religion

The Ideal before Plato

Chapter II: The "Golden Age" of Athens 21

The Polis

A School for Hellas

Chapter III: Socrates and Plato 31

Chapter IV: The Ideal in *The Republic*...........................39

The Child of the Good

The Divided Line

The Allegory of the Cave

Chapter V: Hellenism and the Roman Empire..............60

Chapter VI: Plotinus...72

Plotinus on Happiness, Beauty and Love

Chapter VII: Forgetting the Ideal.................................88

Chapter VIII: The Florentine Renaissance.....................94

Chapter IX: Pico and Ficino..102

Chapter X: Platonic Beauty in the Renaissance............115

Michelangelo, Botticelli, Raphael

Chapter XI: Shakespeare, the Cambridge Platonists and Thomas Taylor...128

Chapter XII: The Transcendentalists and Emerson......141

Chapter XIII: The Legacy of Transcendentalism...........157

Transcendentalism and Spirituality

Transcendentalism and Education

Transcendentalism and Nature

Transcendentalism and Art

Part II: The Ideal as a Way of Life

Chapter XIV: A Natural History of the Ego.................187

The Nature of the Ego

The History of the Ego

Chapter XV: The Ideal and the Art of Dying.................207

Chapter XVI: The Ideal and the Hero's Quest...............227

Theseus and the Minotaur

The Cave as Hero's Quest

The Myth of Er

Epilogue: The Ideal and the Planet.............................246

GRATITUDES

To the readers of the blog and listeners to the podcast idealinthewest.com, especially those who took the time to write encouraging words.

To Richard G. Geldard for his helpful critiques of the early chapters.

To my wife Leah for her love and support.

Preface: An overview of the Ideal

"You're such an Idealist..."

"In an ideal world...."

"Ideally, we could...."

The influence of "Idealism" has so penetrated our language and our thinking that we don't recognize it as perhaps the oldest continuously-operating philosophical system in the West. Although its influence rises and falls, its conception and articulation of "the Good" continues to shape our beliefs and aspirations. This is not good as opposed to evil, but the absolute source of all beneficence, beauty, and justice.

This book grew out of realization that Western civilization is itself in possession of this spiritual tradition which is every bit as compelling and magnificent as any to be found in the East--not that there's anything wrong with them. But I have found myself at each point along the way in studying it saying "yes" in recognition, feeling kinship with figures who lived hundreds and thousands of years ago. As with all true spiritual writing, I feel they are speaking directly to me at this moment. They make me want to be a better man; to be, in fact, Ideal.

Since its founding by Socrates and Plato over 2500 years ago, "Idealism" has been the rootstock of all Western philosophy. Alfred North Whitehead of course said famously that all Western philosophy consists of a series of footnotes to Plato, and Plato's formulation of the Ideal set the tone for something new and unique in the world. It is rational without being dry; spiritual without being religious; it acknowledges the shortcomings of humans, but also believes they can be as gods.

The aim of this book is to show the Ideal not as an abstract intellectual construct, but as an eternal and ever-present reality that can be known in experience by people everywhere. Many attempts have been made to "define" the Ideal, and many of them will be examined in this series, but they all point to it as the ultimate Reality, eternal, ever-present, imperceptible to the senses, but knowable to the intellect. This is not the intellect in the ordinary sense of the thinking or critical mind, but a "higher" faculty of consciousness suited perfectly to knowing the Ideal, sharing its nature. The Ideal is the source of all the transient objects and thoughts that can be perceived, but these are seen derivative, depending on the Ideal for their existence, therefore being less real. In Plato's formulation, they are mere shadows.

For this reason we will not speak of "Idealism" as a school of thought that can be compared and contrasted with other schools of thought. This too is a limitation. As we will see, Plato's school of the Ideal was not in competition with other schools of thought such as Stoicism or Pythagorianism; although they all had different starting-points they all attempted to transform the lives of their students through study and practical exercises. Plato founded his Academy to to teach the Ideal, but he always returned to its indefinability, saying we cannot speak of the Ideal or the Good itself, but only the child of the Good.

It is not that it is supernatural; it is that we are subspiritual. Underneath all the names that are used for it--the Ideal, the Good, the One, the Over-Soul, yes; God, even--is the consciousness that lives also within each of us. It is the source of all we can see or know, but without the anthropomorphic limitations we place on it. In Plato's memorable phrase, it is "the universal author of all things beautiful and right." Many people have studied it, some have written about it, but a small few have known it first-hand, as

Emerson says, "without mediator or veil." It is their unmistakable voices on which I have centered, attempting to let them speak for themselves. They are not historical writers, but every bit as contemporary as the most recent best-seller.

That said, they all lived in times when the state of the language itself had not fallen into the pedestrianism of present-day popular writing, and they are often working at the verge of what is expressible in words at all. The language is meant to make you fly, not walk, and it may take some rereading to give you lift.

This book began life as a podcast, and so my own words and selections of others' have been chosen with an eye to the ear, so to speak. This follows in a line as old as the Ideal, which started as an oral tradition, and whose proponents have for the most part valued the role of speech in expressing it, from Socrates' dialogues in the marketplace to Emerson's lectures on the Lyceum circuit. They knew the value of the spoken word in penetrating some of the filters of reading alone, and I do recommend that you listen to their recorded words as far as they are available, as well as seek out the good company of like-minded people with whom you can share your own speech.

A note on graphics: to keep costs down, I've included black and white images, but color images can be found at Wikimedia Commons, and some at the Google Art Project: www.googleartproject.com

David A. Beardsley

June 2012

The Ideal in the West

Part 1: A History of The Ideal

Chapter I: The Greek Religious Environment

The "Establishment" Religion

Although the Ideal, as we are defining it, is not a product of the mind of man and is the same for all people at all times, it is worth setting the stage for our examination of it by looking at the conception of the "higher powers" as they manifested in the religious practices of Greece at this time. There is always the "establishment" religion, and always some presence of the Ideal, and frequently they are at odds, based as they are on two fundamentally different attitudes toward the "Divine" and man's relation to it.

The Greeks in general practiced a polytheistic religion derived largely from the account of the gods given in Hesiod's *Theogony*. In his account, the gods were a cast of characters who often resembled irrational and spiteful adolescents--kind of like high school with life-and-death powers. They are immortal--they cannot die--but were born; hence theogony. The undisputed king of the gods was Zeus, who gained that title after an extended battle for control. There also existed a variety of other superhuman creatures in the pantheon--demi-gods, heroes, muses, fates, graces, and monsters. Often they are associated with a particular power; for example, the sea-god Poseidon was also seen as the "earth-shaker," in charge of earthquakes, and Demeter was in charge of grain and the abundance of the harvest. There are others who are metaphorical embodiments of particular virtues or characteristics, such as fear (Phobos) or peace (Eirene).

The presence of all these gods appealed to the basic human need for storytelling. What made them gods were their superhuman powers, not their virtue, and so stories of the actions of the gods flourished, especially when there was sex and violence involved, as there often was. Aphrodite would delight in making male gods especially, even Zeus, consumed by lust and causing them to engage in all manner of deviant sex with other goddesses as well as humans, always producing a child as a consequence. Persephone, daughter of Demeter, was abducted to the underworld by Hades, and as a result of the joint-custody arrangement they work out, crops did not grow while Persephone is in Hades. In the Homeric epics, Iliad and Odyssey, the gods played a crucial role, but more often than not by disrupting human plans or putting them in impossible moral situations.

Often the ill effects such as earthquakes or famine experienced by humans were just byproducts of the gods fighting amongst themselves, and if approached in the proper way, they might spare you from these unintended consequences. For the most part the gods seemed uninterested in the plight of humans, even though humans spent much of their time trying to appease them with prayers and animal sacrifices. In Athens, these rituals became ingrained into the life of the people in the form of major and minor holidays and festivals which often featured mass animal sacrifices, theatrical performances and athletic competitions. Each Athenian home usually contained a small shrine of its own for personal devotions and entreaties; for example, a farmer might have a shrine to Demeter, goddess of grain. Given the relatively tolerant approach of the Athenians to other viewpoints, it may come as a surprise to see the extent to which traditional religion was embedded in the life of the city. Although there was not a priesthood or houses of worship per se, the union of "church" and state was total and barely questioned.

One aspect of the religious tradition which moderns often find baffling is the conception of the afterlife. The god Hades ruled over the kingdom of the underworld, also called Hades, where humans were reduced to mere wraiths and shadows, seemingly regardless of whether they have lived a good life or bad. In a passage often cited in *The Odyssey*, Hades is shown as a place where "...the senseless dead men dwell, mere imitations of perished mortals," one of whom is Achilleus, the hero of the Trojan War. Odysseus, attempting to honor his heroism says: "Achilleus, no man has been more blessed than you, nor ever will be. Before, when you were alive, we Argives honored you as we did the gods, and now in this place you have great authority over the dead. Do not grieve, even in death, Achilleus." But Achilles answers: O shining Odysseus, never try to console me for dying. I would rather follow the plow as thrall to another man, one with no land allotted to him and not much to live on, than to be a king over all the perished dead." (Lattimore translation) The meanest human life is still superior to that of a king over the these dark wraiths.

So as a deep source for storytelling, and as an explanation for why things are the way they are, the presence of myriad gods served a valuable purpose; as a unifying theology it did not. And the tendency of theology is always toward unification. As H.D.F. Kitto says in *The Greeks:*

> But the future of Greek religious thought lay neither with the mythology nor with the Olympian gods nor yet with the more personal 'mystery' religions which were complimentary to the Olympian cults. It lay with the philosophers. The Greek element in Christianity is considerable, and it derives from Plato. The Zeus of Aeschylus, pure and lofty as he is, was yet too much the god of the Greek polis to become the God of mankind, just as the God of the Jews could not become also the god of the Gentiles without considerable change. It was Greek philosophy, notably Plato's conception of the absolute, eternal deity, which prepared the world for the reception of a universal religion.[1]

The Ideal before Plato

Paralleling the establishment religious practices in Magna Graecia, other men--philosophers, "lovers of wisdom"--brought forth descriptions of the Ideal. Although they are usually lumped together under the rather condescending title of "Pre-Socratics," each brings a different perspective and personal experience to the study. Some came from a perspective of *phusis,* "physics," or the study of the causes behind natural phenomena. Others came from a more poetic or mystical viewpoint. But all were led to a vision of an *arché,* or first principle, the source of what can be observed in the world of *phusis,* or of *nous,* the mind.

Their formulations of this first principle prepared the ground in which Socrates and Plato could flourish.

In contrast to the "cast of characters," the descriptions of the philosophical tradition are notable for their lack of human traits. Although they may differ somewhat in details, and insofar as the indescribable can be described, what comes through is a vision of pure Being: eternal, changeless, self-contained, all-powerful. That so many different descriptions from so many different authors endured is a testament to how seriously it was taken and how far its influence spread. Even when quoted by much later authors, these fragments speak to a common experience of people living in different times and places: an experience of unity and bliss.

Just as the accounts given by the Presocratics agree in their overall description, it is also worth noting the similarities to Eastern philosophy, particularly the Vedic traditions of India.[2] To oversimplify: the One Reality, the Brahman, is eternal, unchanging, all-blissful, while the world of the senses, Maya, is an illusion, transient, constantly changing, and consequently full of sorrow. As we shall see, this is perfectly congruent with the descriptions given by many who preceded Socrates, as well as Socrates himself. And while the normal tendency of the mind is to look for instances of direct contact between these cultures, brought about by trade or exploration, it is perfectly reasonable to expect that something whose nature is eternal and all-pervasive would appear the same to individuals regardless of geography or history. The Katha Upanishad says, "The Self-existent

Lord pierced the senses to turn outward. Thus we look to the world outside and see not the Self within us. A sage withdrew his sense from the world of change and, seeking immortality, looked within and beheld the deathless Self."[3] This is what the sage always sees regardless of when or where he looks within.

We will never know who was the first sage in the West to have this realization, but it hardly matters. The names we do have show that there was a long and vibrant "counter-cultural" tradition, and the one name most often cited as first was Thales of Miletus (c. 625- c. 545 BC), who founded a tradition of thinkers to come out of this town in the Greek colony of Ionia in Asia Minor. As with all the figures who came before the writing of history had become a science, many of the stories about him are legends and impossible to prove, but there is a consensus that he was among the first to explore natural phenomena without reference to the Hesiodic gods. He observed (some say predicted) an eclipse of the sun in the year 585, which he said was caused by the moon moving in front of it. He is also said to have made studies of magnetism, electricity, and geometry. But despite his pioneering work in giving explanations based on observation, he also searched for primary causes (he thought everything derived from water), and is credited with the phrase *"panta pleure theon"*--"everything is full of gods." While this may seem like a reversion to the accepted theology, it is subtly different. As Werner Jaeger says in *The Theology of the Early Greek Philosophers,* "The assertion that everything is full of gods would then mean something like this: everything is full of mysterious living forces; the distinction between animate and inanimate nature has no foundation in fact; everything has a soul. Thales would thus have made his observation of magnetism a premise for inferring the Oneness of all reality as something alive."[4]

> A similar sentiment is also found in Kitto:
> ...most significant of all is the fact that he assumed, in spite of appearances, that the world consists not of many things but of one. Here we meet a permanent feature of Greek thought: the universe, both the physical and the moral universe, must be not only rational, and therefore knowable, but also simple; the apparent multiplicity of physical things is only superficial.[5]

With the standard cautions about their ability to be verified, there are also these attributions to Thales from Diogenes Laertius' *The Lives of the Philosophers,* written some 900 years later:

> It is not many words which show an intelligent opinion:
> search out one wise thing
> choose one good thing
> for thus you will stop
> the ceaseless tongues of babbling men.
> When asked what is difficult, he said, "To know yourself."...
> What divine, "What has neither beginning nor end."
> How can we live best and most justly? --
> "If we do not ourselves do the things we blame others for doing."
> The motto "Know thyself" is his.... [6]

What is seen here is a kind of democracy brought to the spiritual world. For Thales and his followers, our lives are not subject to the whims of autocratic gods; they are under our own control. Rather than sacrifices, we need knowledge, in particular of ourselves. To be happy--indeed to be godlike--we need to "choose one good thing," and "not ourselves do the things we blame others for doing."

This theme is carried forward in another of the Milesian school--some say he was Thales' student, others that he was an "associate"--Anaximander, ca. 610-ca. 540 BC. An observer of the physical world but also a speculator, he expanded on Thales' view of water as the primal substance by declaring that life came from the sea--that men in fact evolved from fish. However, he rejects water, or any other physical substance, as the basis of the physical world, since it could not be the source of other elements of a different nature, such as fire or earth. His solution was something that more closely invokes the Ideal in being without limit. To quote Jaeger again, " So the thing with which the world begins can only be something that is identical with none of its given substances, and yet is capable of giving rise to the immensity of them all. The distinguishing property of this something must therefore be the fact that it is itself unbounded; and so Anaximander calls it by this very name-- *apeiron*."[7] As far as I can determine, this is the first recorded example in Western thought of a power that is unlimited and indestructible.

Aristotle, in his *Physics*, also specifically mentions Anaximander in conjunction with this idea. "Again, it (the boundless) is ungenerated and indestructible and so is a principle. For what has come into being must have an end, and there is an ending to every destruction. Hence, as I say, it has no principle but itself is thought to be a principle for everything else and to encompass everything and to steer everything--as is said by those who do not set up any other cause (for example mind, or love) apart from the limitless. And it is also the divine; for it is immortal and indestructible, as Anaximander and most of the natural scientists say."[6]

These qualities are also reiterated by another Ionian, Melissus of Samos[7], whose dates are uncertain, but who was contemporary with Socrates. He also adds the logically consistent quality of unity to the limitless: "In this way, then, it is eternal and limitless and one and altogether similar to itself. And it will neither perish nor become larger nor change its arrangement nor suffer pain nor suffer anguish. For if it undergoes any of these things it will no longer be one."[8]

Despite being from Samos, Melissus is usually categorized along with the other main Presocratic school, the Eleatics, named after the town (now called Velia) in Southern Italy where they were centered. Most of the names associated with this school were in fact from Ionia, including Pythagoras of Samos, who established a philosophical community in Sicily, and these emigrants brought with them its inquisitive nature and rejection of the official religion. Southern Italy and Sicily, as the "wild west" of Magna Graecia may have been more tolerant of these "heresies" than the more established colonies in the Aegean.

The seminal figure in this school is Xenophanes, c. 570-c. 475, who left his Ionian home town of Colophon after it was conquered and led a life as a traveling poet in his adopted region after that. He openly satirized the anthropomorphic gods of Hesiod and Homer, pointing out how humans tend to create gods in their own image. But he is not an atheist; in fact, he follows the Ionian school in his depiction of one transcendent reality. "There is one god, among gods and men the greatest, not at all like mortals in body or mind. He sees as a whole, thinks as a whole, and hears as a whole. But without toil he sets everything in motion, by the thought of his mind. And he always remains in the same place, not moving at all, nor is it fitting for him to change his position at different times."[9]

Xenophanes was probably known to the man who has become known as the founder of the Eleatics, Parmenides, but it is unknown whether they had direct contact. Parmenides' dates are uncertain, but place him around the turn of the 5th century, so there would have been overlap with Xenophanes, (as well as Socrates on the other side of his life, if we believe Plato's dialogue bearing Parmenides' name). He carries the vision of Xenophanes even further, eliminating all references to perception and even thought: his conception is that of pure Being. As Richard G. Geldard says in *Parmenides and the Way of Truth,* "Parmenides revealed for the first time a vision of Being not confounded with human attributes. He invented ontology, the philosophy of Being."[10] Parmenides' approach is unique in that it is a reasoned account set within the context of a divine poetic revelation, combining the mystical with the rational.

This poem, of which we now have only fragments of a much-longer work, describes a meeting with a goddess who instructs him first in the way of Truth and then the way of Opinion. He is transported to this meeting in a chariot drawn by a feminine force: "wise mares" guided by "girls, daughters of the sun." They pass through the "gates of Day and Night," transcending this duality to the light. Thus he uses the language and imagery of the conventional religion to transcend it. And we see a reversal of the model of Hesiod: in *Theogony* the goddesses descend (and condescend) to him, but Parmenides is taken to the realm of the goddesses--perhaps the first example of a human penetrating the sphere of the divine.

The goddess first instructs him in the nature of Truth, which sounds a lot like the *apeiron* in its unity and permanence:

One story, one road, now
is left: that it *is*. And on this there are signs
   aplenty that, being, it is ungenerated and
   indestructible,
whole, of one kind and unwavering and
   complete.
Nor was it ever, nor will it be, since now it is, all
   together,
one, continuous.

While Being is, and cannot not be, non-being is not, and cannot be. This sounds obvious, but in our everyday lives of sense perceptions, we believe that things come into being, live for a time, and then pass into non-being--that is they are born and then die. But Parmenides asks:

How might what is then perish? How might it
   have come into being?
For if it came into being it is not, nor if it is ever
      going to be.
Thus generation is quenched and perishing
   unheard of.

After finishing the discourse on Truth, the goddess presents him with a description of opinion, with the words, "Here I cease for you the warranted account and thought about the truth. Henceforward learn mortal opinions, listening to the deceitful arrangement of my words." The natural question which arises is why we should want to listen to "deceitful" words, but Parmenides' objective seems to be to help us discriminate the changeless Being from the limited accounts given in the official religions. As Jaeger says, "To Parmenides our world of Becoming is mere appearance; the world of Being is truth itself. He has no intention that his doctrine of the Existent should explain the natural world of multiplicity and motion; but in his remarkable doctrine of the world of appearance he endeavors to explain the errors of those men who have put duality in place of the One as the primal substance, and motion in place of that which persists unchanged."[11]

This error, he goes on to describe, is a product of the human mind--"mortals who know nothing wander, two-headed"-- and is steeped in duality:
For they determined in their minds to name two forms,
One of which they should not--and that is where they have erred.
And they distinguished them as opposite in kind and set up signs
for them separately from one another: here the ethereal fire of flame,
gentle, very light, in every direction the same as itself
and not the same as the other; and that too, by itself,
opposite--unknowing night, dense in kind, and heavy.
All this plausible arrangement I recount to you
so that no mortal may ever outstrip you in knowledge.

Most of what followed has been lost, but it is clear from this much that we have been plunged into the sensory world of multiplicity and change, becoming and ceasing. The last three lines as preserved by Simplicius read:

> Thus, according to opinion, these things sprang up and now are,
>
> and then, hereafter, having been nourished they will cease to be:
>
> and on them men have set names, a mark for each.

Another of the Presocratic fraternity whose name has almost become is synonym for change is Heraclitus. He is probably most associated with the idea of "flux," that all things are constantly changing, that we can never step into the same river twice. But a closer reading of his work suggests that he was actually in the camp of Being, and that the movements he saw were examples of the the Being transforming itself. At the heart of his epigrammatic writing--which is often opaque and filled with wordplay--is the idea of the *Logos* (the Word or account), and of unity, which he often portrays as meaning the same thing. "Listening not to me, but to the account, it is wise to agree that all things are one." Jaeger says, "Heraclitus always keeps coming back to this one point. The unity of all things is his alpha and omega."[12]

The two streams of *phusis* and *poesis* come together in the person of Empedocles (c.495-c.430?), a native of the town of Akragas (today Agrigento) in Sicily. He seems to have come from a distinguished family, but as with many of these historical figures the legends may have overtaken the facts, so it is not worth dwelling on them. What we have are two poems, or perhaps two sections of one poem, with his speculations on the nature of the physical world, as well as his own report that he was a physician; hence he does seem to straddle these two worlds in a unique way. But let us remember that the main thrust of all the thinkers we have examined was the pursuit of unity, and the divisions that we expect between *phusis* and *poesis* are the artificial products of centuries of deductive thought; for the Presocratics, induction was key, brought together in the unlimited sphere of the divine. Of Empedocles Jaeger says, "In the mythical space of a world pervaded with divine figures, the two attitudes so irreconcilable from our abstract point of view will be seen to fit together as two distinct, but in the last analysis basically homogeneous, spheres for the interplay of divine forces."[13]

Empedocles is credited with developing the classic division of the physical world into the four elements (he calls them "roots") of earth, air, fire and water. These are under the influence of the opposite forces of Love (*philia*) and Strife (*neikos*), which is responsible for the seeming changes of becoming perceptible to the senses. Love intermixes these elements and strife separates them. Human souls too come under the influence of these forces, which he describes in a way that provides an allegory for man's lost divinity that we will see later in Plato. In his poem, he announces himself to be a god:

...I, an immortal god, no longer mortal,
travel, honoured by all, as is fitting,
wreathed with ribbons and fresh garlands.
Whenever I enter a thriving town
I am revered by men and women.

They follow me
in their thousands, asking where lies the path
    to gain:
some want prophecies, others for diseases
of every sort demand to hear a healing word.

But at some point, apparently under the influence of Strife, man forgets his divinity and is condemned to wander, alienated from his godlike nature, in the world of matter.

There is an oracle of necessity, and ancient decree of the gods,

That whenever anyone errs and defiles in fear his dear limbs--

one of the spirits who have been allotted long-lasting life--

he shall wander thrice ten thousand seasons far from the blessed ones.

Such is the road I now follow, and exile from the gods and a wanderer.

He also explicitly acknowledges the immortality of the soul and the transience of the body--"The soul puts its bodies on and off as a man changes his shirt." (Jaeger)--and is responsible for choosing what it will become, a theme that will be seen in Plato's Myth of Er. And he also describes the material world as a "roofed cave," an image that will also be taken up by Plato in *The Republic*.

Anaxagoras, (c.500-428BC), whose dates are roughly the same as those of Empedocles, came from Ionia but moved to Athens around the year 460, establishing a tradition of philosophy in a city which had been preoccupied with war and reconstruction.

His outlook is in the *phusis* camp of Ionia, but his teaching went further than that of Empedocles, saying that the material world is composed not just of four elements, but smaller, undifferentiated particles-- something approaching atoms. " Together were all things, limitless both in quantity and in smallness--for the small too was limitless." But like Empedocles, he postulates the existence of something not material which is necessary to order the basic stuff of the world, a something he calls Thought or Mind (*nous*). "All things were together. Then thought came and arranged them." And later:

> Thought is something limitless and independent, and it has been mixed with no thing but is alone by itself. For if it were not by itself but had been mixed with some other thing, it would share in all things, if it had been mixed with any. For in everything there is present a portion of everything, as I have said earlier. And what was mingled with it would have prevented it from having power over anything in the way in which it does, being in fact alone by itself. For it is the finest of all things and the purest, and it possesses all knowledge about everything, and it has the greatest strength. And thought has power over all those things, both great and small, which possess soul. And thought has power over the whole revolution, so that it revolved in the first place.

Because of his insistence the Mind was the first cause of everything, Anaxagoras was given the nickname of *Nous*. By all accounts kindly and generous, he became a teacher of Pericles and an associate of the playwright Euripides and the sculptor and architect Phidias. He was however forced into exile in the last years of his life, and was received with honors in the town of Lampsacus in the Troad region of what is now Turkey. One of his last wishes was "...that the children have a holiday each year in the month of my death," a wish that was observed for many years.

Anaxagoras left a student by the name of Archelaus, Athens' first homegrown philosopher, of whom little is known except that by some accounts he became the teacher of Socrates.

[1]H.D.F. Kitto, *The Greeks,* Penguin Books, 1991, p. 202-3

[2]This subject has been explored quite thoroughly in Thomas McEviley's *The Shape of Ancient Thought,* Allworth Press, 2001

[3]Eknath Easwaran, trans., *The Upanishads*, Nilgiri Press, 1987, p. 90

[4]Werner Jaeger, *The Theology of the Early Greek Philosophers (The Gifford Lectures),* Wipf and Stock, 2003, p. 21

[5]Diogenes Laertius, quoted in Jonathan Barnes, Early Greek Philosophy, Penguin Classics, 1987, p. 15ff.

[6]Jaeger, op. cit., p. 24

[7]Artistotle, quoted in Barnes, op. cit., p. 22

[8]Not much is known of his life, except that according to Plutarch, he was also a general of the Samian navy and defeated the navy of Pericles in a battle in 441.

[9]Quoted in Barnes, op. cit., p. 96 All other philosopher quotes in Barnes unless otherwise specified.

[10]Quoted in Richard G. Geldard, *Parmenides and the Way of Truth,* Monkfish, 2007, p. 5

[11]Jaeger, op. cit., p. 106

[12]Ibid, p. 123

[13]Ibid. p. 134

Chapter II: The "Golden Age" of Athens

Athens. Ἀθῆναι. Twenty-five centuries ago, depending on who you were, that name would inspire pride, fear, devotion, or rage. Fueled by pride from having repelled an invasion by the seemingly invincible Persians, Athens embarked on a course of action that would make it the first great Western city. Its hubris would result in disaster, but not before it gave birth to one of the most enduring philosophies in the world.

Picking a point at which to begin a history is rather like stepping into the flux of Heraclitus' river: it necessarily ignores all the water that's gone on downstream and has defined the river's shape and depth and banks. But for our purposes, the year 480 BC is close to a new beginning for Athens. We need not go into the causes or details of its two encounters with the Persian empire; just to know that although Athens and its Greek allies were victorious, the victory came at a terrible price. Athens had been conquered by the Persians, its population dispersed, and its defensive walls and most of its buildings destroyed. After its decisive victory over Xerxes at Plataea in 479, Athenians returned to their city to find it in ruins. But with its social structures largely intact and its democratic principles still in effect, its citizens began to rebuild it on a scale unknown to any other city in Europe.

Athens had been one of a number of relatively small city-states that occupied the Greek peninsula. Unlike its arch-rival Sparta, it was a seagoing culture, well-known for its fast and versatile triremes that sailed all around the Mediterranean Sea, establishing and trading with the colonies of Magna Graecia. It took its wine and olives and wheat to the Near East, to Egypt and to Italy, engaged in mostly ceremonial wars with its neighbors, and worked on implementing its limited but unique form of democracy. Through its living tradition of poets and singers, it retold itself the stories of its glory years when the Greeks defeated the Trojans in the Iliad, and how brave Odysseus overcame obstacles and temptations to reunite with his wife Penelope.

Athens was the capital of the larger region of Attica, and much of its wealth still came from the land, which was zealously guarded by the powerful families through inheritance and carefully arranged marriages. Although its constitution made its form of democracy unique in the Greek world, there was still an entrenched oligarchy of these wealthy and powerful families. A progressive taxation system collected more from those who had more, and it seems that this was not resented. The wealthy also considered it their duty to support theatrical performances and some building projects. At the top of the social pyramid were the "Pentacosiomedimni," or the 500 bushel men, who were allowed to be generals in the military, and went down to the Thetes, or manual laborers who served as the foot-soldiers and rowers of the triremes.

Those who did not inherit land would find it hard to come by, and had to work as laborers on one of the large estates, or develop a trade such as pottery-making or stone-carving. Since many of these "technes" or skills were also performed by slaves, it could be hard to make a living.[1] But many of the soldiers and rowers who otherwise would have been unemployed by the relative peace were given jobs in one of the first great public works projects as Athens rebuilt her temples and other public buildings. Originally the idea was to leave many of the temples and other public buildings on the Acropolis in ruins, as a reminder of the terrible suffering the city had endured. This idea was overturned, largely due to the efforts of Pericles, and with the need to rebuild the city, these skills were in demand. As trade returned to normal, Athens found itself becoming wealthier by the day.

The Polis

Regardless of wealth and social standing, however, Athenians were committed to the principles of democracy and the idea of the *polis*. In its most literal sense, the word refers just to the political entity of the city-state, but in a larger sense it encompasses the meaning of the commonwealth of the citizens and the entire system of governance. The governing structure was set up so that all citizens had to participate, and the offices were rotated on a frequent basis so that no one person or family could gain too much power. To be a citizen meant being a free (that is, non-slave) male, both of whose parents were Athenian. Ruled out of the process were of course, women, slaves, and resident aliens known as *metics*. The citizenry had been divided into 10 *demes* based largely on geographical location. These were broken down into smaller governing units to handle more localized issues. There were also non-governing offices that regulated weights and measures, as well as the public infrastructure.

This made for a government of perpetual amateurs, but in a sense this is what Athens wanted-- citizens who had spent time in a number of different positions and had a shared duty of serving the polis as a whole. They felt it superior to the kind of tyranny that had once prevailed and which was the norm in most other states. There was not even an office for a single executive such a president. It is true that one individual, such as Pericles, could exert an outsized influence on events for an extended period, but his office was just that of one of ten generals, and he had to stand for election along with everyone else. He was certainly not immune to criticism and could not prevent some of his associates such as the philosopher Anaxagoras and the sculptor Phidias from being sent into exile.

The two institutions that were at the heart of the democracy were the Assembly, where major laws and policies were debated and voted on, and the law courts where citizens could bring their grievances to be decided by a jury of other citizens. The Assembly's schedule and itinerary were decided by a smaller Council which met in advance, but when it convened with the words "Who wishes to speak?" any citizen had the right to address it. It was of course easier to attend sessions of the Assembly if you had the kind of leisure that came from wealth, but the Thetes and others of lower status were attuned to attempts by the oligarchs to tip the scales in their own favor.

In the law courts, the flip side of the lawmaking process, a citizen could also bring a case against any other citizen, but with several interesting distinctions from our modern jury system. First, the citizen had to defend himself: there were no lawyers. It is true that the plaintiff and defendant could consult with speechwriters ahead of time, but they still had to present their own case. Second, the juries were much larger--at least 501 for routine cases and this could go to 1001 for more important cases. And lastly there were no appeals: the decision was final. It was of course time-consuming and inefficient, but compared with the more ubiquitous systems of decree or vendetta, it provided very important protections and for the most part prevented the kind of violent ongoing feuds that proved to be such a cancer in so many other societies.

Another advantage of this system was that it placed a high value on the skills of reason and persuasion, things not needed if your dispute is going to be resolved strictly on the basis of force or which family you come from. This is the main reason that teachers of rhetoric--the Sophists--flourished in Athens, even though they were not held in very high esteem. As Pierre Hadot says in *What is Ancient Philosophy?*, "The flourishing of democratic life demanded that its citizens, especially those who wanted to achieve positions of power, have a perfect mastery of language. Up until this point, young people had been trained for the acquisition of excellence (*aretē*) by means of *sunousia*, or nonspecialized contact with the adult world. The Sophists, by contrast, invented education in an artificial environment--a system that was to remain one of the characteristics of our civilization."[2] They promised to teach men how to use language and logic to win their case--even to the extent of making "the worse case seem the better." This in turn helped create an overall atmosphere that was conducive to more "intellectual" pursuits such as philosophical discourse and theatrical performances. Even though both Socrates and Plato voiced their opinions on the limitations of democracy, I believe they both realized that they would not be tolerated as long as they were under any other form of government.[3]

The patron goddess of the city of Athens was of course Athena[4], who was quite mature by comparison to most of the other residents of Olympus. She was a daughter of Zeus, and could appear in several aspects. As Athena Polias, "Athena of the City," she was worshiped by the general citizenry, and in her warlike aspect, Athena Promachos, or "First Fighter," she is depicted wearing a helmet and carrying a spear. She is also associated with wisdom or good judgment (or "crafty thinking" if you are less than generous) and is often represented carrying an owl. And in her aspect as Athena Parthenos, The Virgin, she was honored with the most famous building in Greece then as now: the Parthenon. Designed by Phidias and built in a mere 15 years, it is still a model for the perfection of its proportions and its execution. Around its frieze were colorfully painted bas-relief sculptures showing the triumph of the Athenians over the forces of ignorance, the Centaurs, as well as scenes from the annual procession held in Athena's honor, the PanAthenaia. Originally, the Parthenon contained a huge statue of the goddess, as well as another in the square outside it: the tip of her spear could be seen for miles out to sea.

A School for Hellas

In order to protect itself from future invasions, Athens developed a mutual defense society--a NATO of its day--that included other Greek colonies and cities around the Aegean. This Delian League expected "dues" in the form of ships and sailors, or from those cities too small to supply them, cash. As the League evolved more and more into an empire with Athens at its head, the dues became an onerous burden on some of the smaller cities, and Athens would begin to behave as an imperial power, suppressing rebellions as they arose, often brutally.

Lest we paint too rosy a picture of daily life for the Athenians, it should be noted that life was still a struggle for most, and even the rich could not insulate themselves from much of the unpleasantness. There was no sanitation system, which resulted in foul-smelling air and occasional plagues. The diet was very plain and meat was a luxury which for most citizens was enjoyed only on feast days when the sacrificial animals were roasted and eaten. Houses were small and dark, so much of the civic life was lived outdoors. Women were by law not citizens, and were expected to stay sequestered indoors most all their lives. Their own prospects depended on the kind of marriage that their fathers could arrange for them, which was tied into how big a dowry he could afford.

But still Athens had a vibrancy that most other cities of the time could only envy, and Athenians were second to none in their pride. No better evidence exists than the words of Pericles, excerpted from an oration given at the mass funeral of the Athenians who died in the early years of the Peloponnesian War, which began in 431. As recorded by the historian Thucydides he says,

> Our government does not copy our neighbors', but is an example to them. It is true that we are called a democracy, for the administration is in the hands of the many and not of the few. But while there exists equal justice to all and alike in their private disputes, the claim of excellence is also recognized; and when a citizen is in any way distinguished, he is preferred to public service, not as a matter of privilege, but as the reward of merit. Because of the greatness of our city the fruits of the whole earth flow in upon us; so that we enjoy the goods of other countries as freely as our own....Our city is thrown open to the world, though, and we never expel a foreigner and prevent him from seeing or learning anything of which the secret if revealed to an enemy might profit him. ...We alone do good to our neighbors not upon a calculation of interest, but in the confidence of freedom and in a frank and fearless spirit. To sum up: I say that Athens is the school of Hellas, and that the individual Athenian in his own person seems to have the power of adapting himself to the most varied forms of action with utmost versatility and grace.

Within a couple of years however, this bright shining vision of itself was in tatters, from reasons that Pericles could not have foreseen. It is a truism now well-known and exploited by politicians that during wartime the population tends to become more conservative, but at this time it may be one reason that Pericles' adviser Anaxagoras was charged with impiety in 430 and forced into exile; thus Pericles lost a trusted voice of reason. Also, Pericles' strategy for dealing with attacks by the Spartans was not to fight them on land, but to bring the citizens inside the city walls and rely on trade and food from the sea for sustenance. How this unique experiment in non-violent resistance would have affected the history of the world will not be known. In part because of the large increase of people within the city walls, a plague swept through the city in 430-429, claiming about a third of the population, including Pericles. A breakdown in social order followed, documented by Thucydides, with bodies piled up in the streets waiting for cremation and a populace withdrawing into survival mode. Pericles' long-term visionary leadership was replaced by a series of weak and ineffectual rulers. Although there were short-term recoveries, Athens had begun a long slow decline from which it would not return, and which culminated in its conquest by Sparta in 404.

It was into this period of decline that Plato was born in 428. But frequently bad times make for good philosophy, and we will take a look at Socrates, Plato, and their formulation of the Ideal in the next chapter.

[1]Slavery was a fact of life in all the Greek city-states, and the capture of slaves was seen as a normal spoil of war. The wealthiest men could afford hundreds, even thousands of slaves, and it was a very poor man who did not have at least one or two. Most of them labored in the fields or served in the households, and the educated ones tutored the children of their owners.

[2]Pierre Hadot, *What is Ancient Philosophy?*, 2002, Harvard University Press, p. 13

[3]Plato's attempts at establishing an ideal state of his own design, working with the tyrant Dion in Sicily, met with disaster.

[4]Regarding the name of Athena, Socrates says in *Cratylus,* "That is a graver matter, and there, my friend, the modern interpreters of Homer may, I think, assist in explaining the view of the ancients. For most of these in their explanations of the poet, assert that he meant by Athene "mind" (nous) and "intelligence" (dianoia), and the maker of names appears to have had a singular notion about her; and indeed calls her by a still higher title, "divine intelligence" (Thou noesis), as though he would say: This is she who has the mind of God (Theonoa);- using "a" as a dialectical variety "e", and taking away "i" and "s." Perhaps, however, the name Theonoe may mean "she who knows divine things" (Theia nousa) better than others. Nor shall we be far wrong in supposing that the author of it wished to identify this Goddess with moral intelligence (en ethei noesin), and therefore gave her the name ethonoe; which, however, either he or his successors have altered into what they thought a nicer form, and called her Athene."

Chapter III: Socrates and Plato

As we have seen, the basic formulation of a material world, perceptible by the senses but "guided" by an infinite and immortal Being, was well-established by the time of Socrates. But with Socrates and his pupil Plato, it is expanded and takes on an ethical character that has not been seen before.

Socrates (left, gesturing) and Plato (right, pointing up), from "The School of Athens," by Raphael, 1505

Socrates was born in 469 BC, and his life followed the arc of Athens in that glorious and tragic era. The actual details of his life are rather sketchy. He seems to have come from a working-class family, and like most young men of the time, he served in the military, taking part in several campaigns. There are accounts that state he fought bravely, and gained notoriety among his comrades for being able to put up with the cold and lack of food that sometimes were part of the soldier's life. He was 22 when the Parthenon was begun.

He never wrote anything himself, and seemed to hold writing in rather low esteem, as we can tell from this passage, written by Plato, in a dialogue entitled the Phaedrus:

> Socrates: I cannot help feeling, Phaedrus, that writing is unfortunately like painting; for the creations of the painter have the attitude of life, and yet if you ask them a question they preserve a solemn silence. And the same may be said of speeches. You would imagine that they had intelligence, but if you want to know anything and put a question to one of them, the speaker always gives one unvarying answer. And when they have been once written down they are tumbled about anywhere among those who may or may not understand them, and know not to whom they should reply, to whom not: and, if they are maltreated or abused, they have no parent to protect them; and they cannot protect or defend themselves.
>
> Phaedrus. That again is most true.
>
> Socrates: Is there not another kind of word or speech far better than this, and having far greater power--a son of the same family, but lawfully begotten?
>
> Phaedrus. Whom do you mean, and what is his origin?
>
> Socrates: I mean an intelligent word graven in the soul of the learner, which can defend itself, and knows when to speak and when to be silent.
>
> Phaedrus. You mean the living word of knowledge which has a soul, and of which a written word is properly no more than an image?
>
> Socrates: Yes, of course that is what I mean.[1]

Everyone ever since who has written about Socrates, including no doubt Plato when he wrote those words, has probably felt the sting of this irony. But we see here an early indication of the distinction he makes between something real, that is with a soul, and something that is a mere image of that reality.

There is no account of when and why he started practicing philosophy, but he does seem to have been a student for a time of Archelaus who was in turn a student of Anaxagoras. In the dialog called the *Symposium*, Plato has Socrates say that he learned about love and beauty from a priestess from Mantineia named Diotima. He quotes her as telling him, "But what if man had eyes to see the true beauty —the divine beauty, I mean, pure and clear and unalloyed, not clogged with the pollution of mortality, and all the colors and vanities of human life, thither looking, and holding converse with the true beauty divine and simple, and bringing into being and educating true creations of virtue and not idols only? Do you not see that in that communion only, beholding beauty with the eye of the mind, he will be enabled to bring forth, not images of beauty, but realities....."

The kind of philosophy Socrates is shown to espouse is not then a body of theoretical knowledge or rhetorical devices such as those practiced by the Sophists, but rather an expression of a self-existent source of "all things beautiful and right." In his book *Shakespeare and Platonic Beauty,*[2] John Vyvyan says, "Considered philosophically, love and beauty were invented by Plato. And whenever the European mind has theorized about them since--until the Freudians set a cat among the pigeons--some echo of the Symposium or the Phaedrus is nearly always to be caught." For Plato, these qualities are built in to the Ideal; they are not afterthoughts.

He felt it was possible for humans to come to knowledge of this source through the practice of asking questions with the aim of finding the truth about a certain subject. Plato called this practice "dialectic," a "talking through," and it allowed Socrates to claim that he knew nothing and to deflate those who claimed they did know something. In a number of dialogs, he is shown engaging with and annoying the professional Sophists who claimed to teach wisdom for a price.

As described by Plato, Socrates usually spent his days in the Agora, the marketplace, in dialog with anyone who wanted to talk--and often those who did not. It is not known how he made a living at this, even though he was married and had three sons. But in addition to Plato, he did have a number of devoted students who no doubt found ways to support him and his family short of outright payment for services.

The Athens into which Plato was born in 428, as we've seen, was a very different place. Shortly before his birth, the city was ravaged by a plague that killed perhaps a third of the population, including Pericles, just at the time Athens entered into a new phase of war with Sparta and the Peloponnesian League. In 416 Athens armed a huge fleet with the intent of conquering Sicily, but the adventure ended in disaster a couple of years later with the entire force dead or sold into slavery. Athens fought on, but in 404 was forced to surrender to Sparta. The Golden Age of boundless ambition had ended in defeat.

In an act of extreme humiliation, the democracy was overthrown by the Spartans and a tyranny installed. Although the democracy was reestablished shortly after, Athens' sense of invincibility had been shattered, and religious and political conservatism grew stronger. In this environment, in 399 BC, Socrates was brought up on the same charge of impiety that had been brought against Anaxagoras some 30 years before. Specifically he was accused of "introducing new gods, and of corrupting the young." As we've seen, the Greeks worshiped many gods and sought through sacrifices and offerings to bend the fickle gods' will in their favor. Socrates, while using the language of these gods, like Anaxagoras essentially taught the existence of one supreme Being, the unchanging Form of the Good, and in that respect he was guilty as charged. But it is to their shame that the Greeks reverted to the false comfort of their traditional gods, and condemned Socrates to death.

As described in the dialog called the *Phaedo*, Socrates argued for the immortality of the soul and had no fear of death. He drank the prescribed hemlock rather than escape prison, and believed, in fact, that he was escaping the prison of the body. He told his followers who had gathered in his cell, "In this present life, I reckon that we make the nearest approach to knowledge when we have the least possible concern or interest in the body, and are not saturated with the bodily nature, but remain pure until the hour when God himself is pleased to release us. And then the foolishness of the body will be cleared away and we shall be pure and hold converse with other pure souls, and know of ourselves the clear light everywhere; and this is surely the light of truth." The analogy of the truth as light is one we will encounter again and again in Plato and his heirs.

Plato came from an aristocratic family, and was given the appropriate name Aristocles—Plato is a nickname. One account has it that he planned to be a tragic playwright, but upon meeting Socrates about 407 BC, he gave up that idea to devote himself to philosophy. The story perhaps helps us to understand the dialog format chosen by Plato for most of his works—they are almost always in the form of people in conversation; perhaps his attempt to reconcile Socrates' distrust of writing with his own desire to make Socrates' teachings last. Except for a few ill-fated trips abroad, Plato lived in Athens for all of his life; did not marry, and left no children. He did, however, found a school--the Academy--to carry on the teachings of Socrates, which lasted until the 6th century AD and was guided by the principle "Know Thyself." It was unique among the several philosophical schools of the time in that it also accepted women as students.

Plato wrote extensively, on a wide variety of philosophical subjects, but he also seems to have believed as did Socrates, that the written word has its limitations, and that true philosophy can only be communicated through face-to-face study and conversation. In his work called the Seventh Letter, he writes, "For it does not admit of exposition like other branches of knowledge; but after much converse about the matter itself and a life lived together, suddenly a light, as it were, is kindled in one soul by a flame that leaps to it from another, and thereafter sustains itself."

Unlike many philosophers of the period, a large body of Plato's works has survived, and has been endlessly debated and analyzed. It is not the purpose of this book to enter into that discussion. Rather we will center on what is perhaps his most enduring contribution to philosophy: what he called "the ideal of the Good," the Ἀγάθων (*agathon*). He speaks of it in several works, but most thoroughly and beautifully in one of his longest works, written about 380 BC: The Republic.

[1]There are many editions of all Plato's works, and a good online source for all, in translation by Benjamin Jowett, is The Perseus Project at:

http://www.perseus.tufts.edu/hopper/

[2]John Vyvyan, *Shakespeare and Platonic Beauty,* Chatto & Windus, 1961 This book has just been reprinted by Forgotten Books (forgottenbooks.org), which also offers it as a free download. It is obviously just scanned from an original 1961 version, but is at least available.

It's also available (with many Optical Character Recognition errors) at:

http:www.archive.org/details/shakespeareandpl00151 0mbp

Chapter IV: The Ideal in *The Republic*

The events of "The Republic" take place in Athens' port city, called the Piraeus, about a five mile walk from the Acropolis. Not that there are that many events; as narrated by Socrates, he goes down to the Piraeus to see a festival in the company of Glaucon, who is the brother of Plato. They are ready to return to Athens when they are stopped by a young man named Polemarchus and Plato's other brother Adeimantus. Soon they fall into a discussion of the nature of justice, considering what makes a just person and a just state, and the rest of the book is an account of a major all-nighter in which this question is examined in detail. While most interpreters focus on the political implications of the the work, it is worth remembering that Socrates makes it clear that justice and wisdom cannot be just functions of the state; they must exist in the individual as well. The state is the citizen writ large.

Now the politics of the Republic has been debated and analyzed endlessly since it appeared, and we won't be entering into that territory. But about midway through the book, Plato has Socrates make the remarkable statement that perfect justice cannot be established in the state (or the individual) until philosophers become the rulers. And to be true philosophers he says, they must be schooled in "the highest knowledge."

His interlocutor, Adeimantus, rightly asks, "... do you suppose that we shall refrain from asking you what is this highest knowledge?" To which Socrates replies,

> Nay, I said, ask if you will; but I am certain that you have heard the answer many times, and now you either do not understand me or, as I rather think, you are disposed to be troublesome; for you have been told that the idea of good is the highest knowledge, and that all other things become useful and advantageous only by their use of this. You can hardly be ignorant that of this I was about to speak, concerning which, as you have often heard me say, we know so little; and, without which, any other knowledge or possession of any kind will profit us nothing. Do you think that the possession of all other things is of any value if we do not possess the good? or the knowledge of all other things if we have no knowledge of beauty and goodness?

Well, of course not. But when Adeimantus and Glaucon press him further, Socrates says that he cannot speak of the Good itself, but he can describe "the child of the Good." He goes on to use three different analogies to describe it.

The Child of the Good

The first description he uses is the analogy of the sun, which makes the distinction between the world of visible things and the world of invisible ideas.

> Socrates: ...there is an absolute beauty and an absolute good, and of other things to which the term 'many' is applied there is an absolute; for

they may be brought under a single idea, which is called the essence of each.

Glaucon: Very true.

The many, as we say, are seen but not known, and the ideas are known but not seen.

Exactly.

And what is the organ with which we see the visible things?

The sight, he said.

And with the hearing, I said, we hear, and with the other senses perceive the other objects of sense?

True.

But have you remarked that sight is by far the most costly and complex piece of workmanship which the artificer of the senses ever contrived?

No, I never have, he said.

Then reflect; has the ear or voice need of any third or additional nature in order that the one may be able to hear and the other to be heard?

Nothing of the sort.

No, indeed, I replied; and the same is true of most, if not all, the other senses --you would not say that any of them requires such an addition?

Certainly not.

But you see that without the addition of some other nature there is no seeing or being seen?

How do you mean?

Sight being, as I conceive, in the eyes, and he who has eyes wanting to see; color being also present in them, still unless there be a third nature specially adapted to the purpose, the owner of the eyes will see nothing and the colors will be invisible.

Of what nature are you speaking?

Of that which you term light, I replied.

True, he said.

Noble, then, is the bond which links together sight and visibility, and great beyond other bonds by no small difference of nature; for light is their bond, and light is no ignoble thing?

Nay, he said, the reverse of ignoble.

And which, I said, of the gods in heaven would you say was the lord of this element? Whose is that light which makes the eye to see perfectly and the visible to appear?

You mean the sun, as you and all mankind say.

May not the relation of sight to this deity be described as follows?

How?

Neither sight nor the eye in which sight resides is the sun?

No.

Yet of all the organs of sense the eye is the most like the sun?

By far the most like.

And the power which the eye possesses is a sort of effluence which is dispensed from the sun?

Exactly.

Then the sun is not sight, but the author of sight who is recognized by sight.

True, he said.

And this is he whom I call the child of the good, whom the good begat in his own likeness, to be in the visible world, in relation to sight and the things of sight, what the good is in the intellectual world in relation to mind and the things of mind.

Will you be a little more explicit? he said.

Why, you know, I said, that the eyes, when a person directs them towards objects on which the light of day is no longer shining, but the moon and stars only, see dimly, and are nearly blind; they seem to have no clearness of vision in them?

Very true.

But when they are directed towards objects on which the sun shines, they see clearly and there is sight in them?

Certainly.

And the soul is like the eye: when resting upon that on which truth and being shine, the soul perceives and understands and is radiant with intelligence; but when turned towards the twilight of becoming and perishing, then she has opinion only, and goes blinking about, and is first of one opinion and then of another, and seems to have no intelligence?

Just so.

Now, that which imparts truth to the known and the power of knowing to the knower is what I would have you term the idea of good, and this you will deem to be the cause of science, and of truth in so far as the latter becomes the subject of knowledge; beautiful too, as are both truth and knowledge, you will be right in esteeming this other nature as more beautiful than either; and, as in the previous instance, light and sight may be truly said to be like the sun, and yet not to be the sun, so in this other sphere, science and truth may be deemed to be like the good, but not the good; the good has a place of honor yet higher.

What a wonder of beauty that must be, he said, which is the author of science and truth, and yet surpasses them in beauty; for you surely cannot mean to say that pleasure is the good?

God forbid, I replied; but may I ask you to consider the image in another point of view?

In what point of view?

You would say, would you not, that the sun is not only the author of visibility in all visible things, but of generation and nourishment and growth, though he himself is not generation?

Certainly.

In like manner the good may be said to be not only the author of knowledge to all things known, but of their being and essence, and yet the good is not essence, but far exceeds essence in dignity and power.

Glaucon said, with a ludicrous earnestness: By the light of heaven, how amazing!

So Glaucon doesn't get it, of course, but Socrates is saying that the Good is the source of our ability to think and be conscious at all, just as the sun is the source of our ability to see. "The light of heaven" indeed. The sun in effect is the source of the eye as well as the things seen by the eye, however imperfectly. The good is in effect the source of the mind as well as all the mind-things it perceives, however imperfectly. But just as we are not ordinarily aware of the sun or artificial light source—we just think we see things—we are not aware of the Good as the source of knowledge and essence. We just think we think. The critical mind, magnificent as it is, is just an effect in this continuum, and plagued by duality, is not equipped to realize the unity of the Ideal.

As things prove the light, so our thoughts prove the consciousness, the ideas the Idea. In this analogy, our thoughts and feelings are the furnishings of the mind--its chairs and tables and paintings. Most self-help programs are aimed at rearranging your furniture, or perhaps getting a decorator to help you upgrade it. The aim of the Ideal is to lift the roof off your house.

The Divided Line

Now Plato goes for a more "left-brain" approach. Some may find it helpful to have a graphic representation of the divided line, and examples abound. But it can also be instructive not to look at a drawing, but to treat the description as an exercise of the "intelligible" rather than the "sensible." For one, it avoids pointless questions like whether the line is vertical or horizontal, or left or right. Also, to do so is an example of using what Plato describes as "that other sort of knowledge which reason herself attains by the power of dialectic, using the hypotheses not as first principles, but only as hypotheses...." If you need to "see" in order to "believe," you are stuck in the sensible end of the line, and will never be able to see light as opposed to things in the light. (That said, this is the most abstract of the descriptions, and an image is helpful—I've included on at the end of the description.)

> Socrates: You have to imagine, then, that there are two ruling powers, and that one of them is set over the intellectual world, the other over the visible. I do not say heaven, lest you should fancy that I am playing upon the name (ουρανος, opatos). May I suppose that you have this

45

distinction of the visible and intelligible fixed in your mind?

I have.

Now take a line which has been cut into two unequal parts, and divide each of them again in the same proportion, and suppose the two main divisions to answer, one to the visible and the other to the intelligible, and then compare the subdivisions in respect of their clearness and want of clearness, and you will find that the first section in the sphere of the visible consists of images. And by images I mean, in the first place, shadows, and in the second place, reflections in water and in solid, smooth and polished bodies and the like: Do you understand?

Yes, I understand.

Imagine, now, the other section, of which this is only the resemblance, to include the animals which we see, and everything that grows or is made.

Very good.

Would you not admit that both the sections of this division have different degrees of truth, and that the copy is to the original as the sphere of opinion is to the sphere of knowledge?

Most undoubtedly.

Next proceed to consider the manner in which the sphere of the intellectual is to be divided.

In what manner?

Thus: There are two subdivisions, in the lower of which the soul uses the figures given by the former division as images; the inquiry can only be hypothetical, and instead of going upward to a principle descends to the other end; in the higher of the two, the soul passes out of hypotheses, and goes up to a principle which is above hypotheses, making no use of images as in the former case, but proceeding only in and through the ideas themselves.

I do not quite understand your meaning, he said.

Then I will try again; you will understand me better when I have made some preliminary remarks. You are aware that students of geometry, arithmetic, and the kindred sciences assume the odd, and the even, and the figures, and three kinds of angles, and the like, in their several branches of science; these are their hypotheses, which they and everybody are supposed to know, and therefore they do not deign to give any account of them either to themselves or others; but they begin with them, and go on until they arrive at last, and in a consistent manner, at their conclusion?

Yes, he said, I know.

And do you not know also that although they make use of the visible forms and reason about them, they are thinking not of these, but of the ideals which they resemble; not of the figures which they draw, but of the absolute square and the absolute diameter, and so on--the forms which they draw or make, and which have shadows and reflections in water of their own, are converted by them into images, but they are really seeking to behold the things themselves, which can only be seen with the eye of the mind?

That is true.

And of this kind I spoke as the intelligible, although in the search after it the soul is

47

compelled to use hypotheses; not ascending to a first principle, because she is unable to rise above the region of hypothesis, but employing the objects of which the shadows below are resemblances in their turn as images, they having in relation to the shadows and reflections of them a greater distinctness, and therefore a higher value.

I understand, he said, that you are speaking of the province of geometry and the sister arts.

And when I speak of the other division of the intelligible, you will understand me to speak of that other sort of knowledge which reason herself attains by the power of dialectic, using the hypotheses not as first principles, but only as hypotheses-- that is to say, as steps and points of departure into a world which is above hypotheses, in order that she may soar beyond them to the first principle of the whole; and clinging to this and then to that which depends on this, by successive steps she descends again without the aid of any sensible object, from ideas, through ideas, and in ideas she ends.

I understand you, he replied; not perfectly, for you seem to me to be describing a task which is really tremendous; but, at any rate, I understand you to say that knowledge and being, which the science of dialectic contemplates, are clearer than the notions of the arts, as they are termed, which proceed from hypotheses only: these are also contemplated by the understanding, and not by the senses: yet, because they start from hypotheses and do not ascend to a principle, those who contemplate them appear to you not to exercise the higher reason upon them, although when a first principle is added to them they are cognizable by the higher reason. And the habit which is concerned with geometry and the cognate sciences I suppose that you would term understanding, and not reason, as being intermediate between opinion and reason.

You have quite conceived my meaning, I said; and now, corresponding to these four divisions, let there be four faculties in the soul--reason (*noesis*) answering to the highest, understanding (*dianoia*) to the second, faith (or conviction) (*pistis*) to the third, and perception of shadows (*eikaisia*) to the last--and let there be a scale of them, and let us suppose that the several faculties have clearness in the same degree that their objects have truth.

I understand, he replied, and give my assent, and accept your arrangement.

The Divided Line
Plato, *The Republic*, Book 6

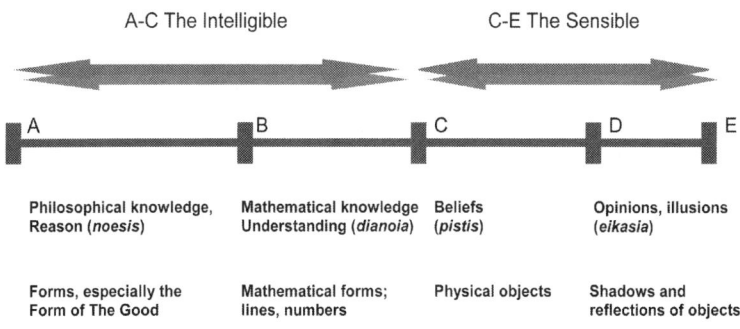

A-C The Intelligible   C-E The Sensible

A   B   C   D   E

Philosophical knowledge, Reason (*noesis*)   Mathematical knowledge Understanding (*dianoia*)   Beliefs (*pistis*)   Opinions, illusions (*eikasia*)

Forms, especially the Form of The Good   Mathematical forms; lines, numbers   Physical objects   Shadows and reflections of objects

So score another one for Socratic irony: Glaucon has just heard something that could have blown the top off his head, that is, the soul has the capacity for contemplation through the faculty of reason which is beyond the understanding. But he contents himself with saying, "I understand...assent...accept." Plato is anticipating the reaction of those who would reduce this teaching to a system that can be "understood" by the critical mind, and then compared and contrasted with other systems. Glaucon is stuck with the hypotheses as ends in themselves, and cannot "soar beyond them to the first principle of the whole...." The term noesis, translated by Jowett as reason, is not the same as reasoning, which is more the realm of dianoia, the discursive mind. Noesis has the meaning of intuitive, a priori, knowledge—higher even than hypotheses. It is the realm of the Ideal, of contemplation, where the very machinery of the discursive mind can be observed.

An objection is sometimes raised that by using the term "divided," that Plato is creating or perpetuating a duality--intelligible vs. visible. But I think this is a product of a dualistic mind, like Glaucon's. Another apt analogy would be that of an electrical grid: there are the generators, transmission lines, wires running throughout the house, and finally the appliances. One can divide this grid up into different parts for convenience sake, but we should not forget that it is all the physical apparatus of the invisible electrical current, whose nature is the same regardless of where on the grid it is located. If the grid here is analogous to the Intelligible realm, we are like intellectual appliances in the visible, and we go along happily thinking we are separate, self-controlling toasters or lamps or microwaves. Until one day our plug gets pulled.

So I believe Plato intends the divided line not as a mere philosophical diagram, but as a description of our true nature, and an aid in ascending the line to reach the *noesis*. In the Symposium, he describes, through Diotima, how someone who wished to see the form of beauty itself should begin by looking as much as possible on beautiful things, and proceed from there to an appreciation of the beauty of the mind and contemplate the beauty of laws and institutions and the sciences-- "the vast sea of beauty."

Diotima says,

And the true order of going, or being led by another, to the things of love, is to begin from the beauties of earth and mount upwards for the sake of that other beauty, using these as steps only, and from one going on to two, and from two to all fair forms, and from fair forms to fair practices, and from fair practices to fair notions, until from fair notions he arrives at the notion of absolute beauty, and at last knows what the essence of beauty is. ...But what if man had eyes to see the true beauty — the divine beauty, I mean, pure and clear and unalloyed, not clogged with the pollutions of mortality and all the colours and vanities of human life — thither looking, and holding converse with the true beauty simple and divine? Remember how in that communion only, beholding beauty with the eye of the mind, he will be enabled to bring forth, not images of beauty, but realities (for he has hold not of an image but of a reality), and bringing forth and nourishing true virtue to become the friend of God and be immortal, if mortal man may. Would that be an ignoble life?

The Allegory of the Cave

The Cave allegory is one of the most analyzed and debated passages in Western philosophy, which of course means bringing the discursive mind to bear on something which is the realm of the noetic. Plato's meaning of the ascent from the realm of ignorance and shadows to the realm of consciousness and knowledge is clear, if we don't try to analyze it. We need also to remember that this is not "Plato's Cave," located somewhere near Athens twenty-five hundred years ago. This is the cave in which you and I spend our lives, entranced by the shadows on the wall. Plato can show us the way out—but first we have to realize he is talking about and to us.

> And now, I said, let me show in a figure how far our nature is enlightened or unenlightened: Behold! human beings living in an underground den, which has a mouth open toward the light and reaching all along the den; here they have been from their childhood, and have their legs and necks chained so that they cannot move, and can only see before them, being prevented by the chains from turning round their heads. Above and behind them a fire is blazing at a distance, and between the fire and the prisoners there is a raised way; and you will see, if you look, a low wall built along the way,

like the screen which marionette-players have in front of them, over which they show the puppets.

I see.

And do you see, I said, men passing along the wall carrying all sorts of vessels, and statues and figures of animals made of wood and stone and various materials, which appear over the wall? Some of them are talking, others silent.

You have shown me a strange image, and they are strange prisoners.

Like ourselves, I replied; and they see only their own shadows, or the shadows of one another, which the fire throws on the opposite wall of the cave?

True, he said; how could they see anything but the shadows if they were never allowed to move their heads?

And of the objects which are being carried in like manner they would only see the shadows?

Yes, he said.

And if they were able to converse with one another, would they not suppose that they were naming what was actually before them?

Very true.

And suppose further that the prison had an echo which came from the other side, would they not be sure to fancy when one of the passers-by spoke that the voice which they heard came from the passing shadow?

No question, he replied.

To them, I said, the truth would be literally nothing but the shadows of the images.

That is certain.

And now look again, and see what will naturally follow if the prisoners are released and disabused of their error. At first, when any of them is liberated and compelled suddenly to stand up and turn his neck round and walk and look toward the light, he will suffer sharp pains; the glare will distress him, and he will be unable to see the realities of which in his former state he had seen the shadows; and then conceive someone saying to him, that what he saw before was an illusion, but that now, when he is approaching nearer to being and his eye is turned toward more real existence, he has a clearer vision--what will be his reply? And you may further imagine that his instructor is pointing to the objects as they pass and requiring him to name them--will he not be perplexed? Will he not fancy that the shadows which he formerly saw are truer than the objects which are now shown to him?

Far truer.

And if he is compelled to look straight at the light, will he not have a pain in his eyes which will make him turn away to take refuge in the objects of vision which he can see, and which he will conceive to be in reality clearer than the things which are now being shown to him?

True, he said.

And suppose once more, that he is reluctantly dragged up a steep and rugged ascent, and held fast until he is forced into the presence of the sun himself, is he not likely to be pained and irritated? When he approaches the light his eyes will be dazzled, and he will not be able to see anything at all of what are now called realities.

Not all in a moment, he said.

He will require to grow accustomed to the sight of the upper world. And first he will see the shadows best, next the reflections of men and other objects in the water, and then the objects themselves; then he will gaze upon the light of the moon and the stars and the spangled heaven; and he will see the sky and the stars by night better than the sun or the light of the sun by day?

Certainly.

Last of all he will be able to see the sun, and not mere reflections of him in the water, but he will see him in his own proper place, and not in another; and he will contemplate him as he is.

Certainly. He will then proceed to argue that this is he who gives the season and the years, and is the guardian of all that is in the visible world, and in a certain way the cause of all things which he and his fellows have been accustomed to behold?

Clearly, he said, he would first see the sun and then reason about him. And when he remembered his old habitation, and the wisdom of the den and his fellow-prisoners, do you not suppose that he would felicitate himself on the change, and pity him?

Certainly, he would.

And if they were in the habit of conferring honors among themselves on those who were quickest to observe the passing shadows and to remark which of them went before, and which followed after, and which were together; and who were therefore best able to draw conclusions as to the future, do you think that he would care for such honors and glories, or envy the possessors of them? Would he not say with Homer,

"Better to be the poor servant of a poor master," *and to endure anything, rather than think as they do and live after their manner?"*

Yes, he said, I think that he would rather suffer anything than entertain these false notions and live in this miserable manner.

Imagine once more, I said, such a one coming suddenly out of the sun to be replaced in his old situation; would he not be certain to have his eyes full of darkness?

To be sure, he said.

And if there were a contest, and he had to compete in measuring the shadows with the prisoners who had never moved out of the den, while his sight was still weak, and before his eyes had become steady (and the time which would be needed to acquire this new habit of sight might be very considerable), would he not be ridiculous? Men would say of him that up he went and down he came without his eyes; and that it was better not even to think of ascending; and if anyone tried to loose another and lead him up to the light, let them only catch the offender, and they would put him to death.

No question, he said.

This entire allegory, I said, you may now append, dear Glaucon, to the previous argument; the prison-house is the world of sight, the light of the fire is the sun, and you will not misapprehend me if you interpret the journey upward to be the ascent of the soul into the intellectual world according to my poor belief, which, at your desire, I have expressed--whether rightly or wrongly, God knows. But, whether true or false, my opinion is that in the world of knowledge the idea of good appears last of all, and is seen only with an effort; and, when seen, is also inferred to be the universal author of all things beautiful and right, parent of light and of the lord of light in this visible world, and the immediate source of reason and truth in the intellectual; and that this is the power upon which he who would act rationally either in public or private life must have his eye fixed.

The quote from Homer to which Socrates alludes is telling: it is from the Odyssey, which recounts the "test and quest myth" of the hero Odysseus and his journey homeward after fighting in the Trojan War. He is beset by trials and temptations as he tries to work his way back to his homeland and wife, Penelope. By analogy, Socrates is saying that we have also traveled far from our true home, and that what is needed is for each of us to become a spiritual Odysseus, to make the soul's journey, from becoming to being, from temporal to eternal, from the partial to the One.

Plato also realizes that "those who attain this beatific vision are unwilling to descend into human affairs; for their souls are ever hastening into the upper world where they desire to dwell...." But he believes it is the duty of the enlightened ones to make the return to the cave and become the philosopher-kings, since only they can administer the state with justice, and their very reluctance to govern is their main qualification for it.

> Whereas the truth is that the State in which the rulers are most reluctant to govern is always the best and most quietly governed, and the State in which they are most eager, the worst.
>
> Quite true, he replied
>
> And will our pupils, when the hear this, refuse to take their turn at the toils of the State, when they are allowed to spend the greater part of their time with one another in the heavenly light?

Because they have "seen the beautiful and just and good in their truth," they can return to their state of enlightenment even while serving as kings.

So this quest is also the one that we must make as individuals to realize the Good within ourselves. All along, of course, Plato has been using the larger State as an analogy for the individual one. Most discussions of the Republic focus on the larger State since looking at ourselves is the kind of uncomfortable examination we try to avoid at all costs. But I think Plato is really talking about our own inner government: how we free the soul from the illusions of the ego and return the philosopher to his rightful kingship.

Our spiritual quest to return to the Good is the true hero's journey, and the true hero's return. It is what Joseph Campbell, quoting James Joyce, calls the monomyth. "A hero ventures forth from the world of common day into a region of supernatural wonder: fabulous forces are there encountered and a decisive victory is won: the hero comes back from this mysterious adventure with the power to bestow boons on his fellow man."[1]

We will be examining the mythological underpinnings of the quest in more detail in the second part of the book. Suffice it to say for now that Plato is saying that our first task as humans is to make this journey out of the cave, to realize the Ideal, and then we are able to see and enjoy the world and the infinite variety and drama of the Ideal, while still spending "the greater part of (our) time with one another in the heavenly light."

[1]Joseph Campbell, *The Hero with a Thousand Faces,* New World Library, 2008

Chapter V: Hellenism and the Roman Empire

The events in the Republic were set around 420 BC, at a time when Athens' grasp on power was already beginning to slip. As we saw, Pericles had died almost a decade before during the great plague that had killed nearly a third of its population. It was in the midst of the war with Sparta and other city-states on the mainland, and was also facing increased rebellions from its colonies on the Aegean. In a few years, its desire for greater empire would lead Athens to invade Sicily, encouraged by Socrates' student Alcibiades, which would end in disaster. Athens fought on, but in 404 it was defeated by Sparta, and the democracy replaced by a Spartan-imposed group of thirty tyrants. In less than a century, Athens had risen from nowhere to become the first great city in the Western world. But in doing so it fell victim to the urge for power that had compelled its own invaders, and would compel others.

With its dreams of expansion crushed, Athens turned back on itself, and looked for scapegoats on whom it could blame its humiliation. One likely candidate was Socrates. To us, Socrates is a revered figure, an archetype of the questioning Western mind. But to many who lived in Athens at this time, he was an annoyance at best, a danger at worst. He himself described his role as that of a gadfly, trying to sting his fellow citizens out of their complacency and preoccupation with wealth and pleasure and power. In the course of doing so, he made many enemies.

In the year 399, when he was 70 years old, Socrates was put on trial, charged with impiety, or introducing new gods, and of corrupting the youth. As mentioned before, insofar as Socrates taught the existence of one supreme being--the Good--he went against the multiple "personal" gods of the Greeks, and was guilty as charged. There is no record of what his accusers said against him, but Socrates' defense is recorded by Plato in *The Apology*. But "apology" here has the meaning of "explanation" or "defense." It has nothing to do with asking forgiveness; in fact, Socrates seems to go out of his way to annoy his judges. It is not surprising then, that they would return a verdict of guilty, and like the prisoners still chained in the cave, sentence him to death.

While verdicts could not be appealed and sentences were usually carried out quickly, Socrates' trial coincided with a ritual to Apollo that involved sending a ship to the island of Delos. While the ship was away, no executions were allowed, so Socrates' students had many opportunities to meet with him, meetings which are appropriately concerned largely with the issues of death and mortality. And just as Socrates has argued that above the physical world of change and decay there is something that is permanent and changeless, he now argues that there is something similarly distinct from the human body: an immortal soul. The philosopher, who has cultivated knowledge of his soul, will not then fear death.

> Socrates: But the soul, the invisible part which has gone to a place which resembles itself in being fine and pure and invisible—quite literally

to the Unseen World—to the good and wise God —to which place, if God wills, my soul too must go very shortly; does our soul, I say, which is of such a form and nature, really get blown away and perish in the very moment of being separated from the body, as most men say? Far from it, dear Cebes and Simmias. The facts are these: let us suppose that it is pure when separated, dragging nothing of the body with it, as having (willfully anyhow) had no dealings with the body during its lifetime, but having shunned it and kept itself to itself, making that its constant aim and practice—which simply means, in fact, pursuing philosophy in the correct manner, and in very truth practicing death; or wouldn't you call this a "practice of death?"

Certainly.

Then in this state it goes away to the place which is like itself, invisible, to that which is divine and and deathless and wise, and when it arrives there it is its lot to be happy, freed from uncertainty and folly and fears and wild desires and all the other ills from which man suffers, and (as is said of those who have been initiated into the Mysteries) in very truth spending the rest of time in company with the gods?[1]

This of course sounds a lot like what we now think of as heaven. But at the time, this was something quite new. In the Greek stories of the gods, they descended into the world of men, but men did not ascend to the level of gods. Parmenides speaks of being carried to this realm in his epic poem, but he is only a sojourner there. Socrates was arguably the first to make this claim: that a human being has a soul that can, through its love of wisdom, ascend to the level of gods and realize eternal happiness.

"The Death of Socrates," by Jacques-Louis David, 1787

At the end of the dialogue, at sunset, when Apollo's ship has returned from Delos, the bowl of hemlock is brought for Socrates to drink. Phaedo describes it this way: "...he raised the cup to his lips, and showing not the least distaste, quite unperturbed, he drained the draught. Most of us had till then been more or less able to restrain our tears, but when we saw him drinking and then that he had drunk it, would do so no longer. For my part, despite my efforts I found that the the tears flooded down my cheeks; I wrapped my face in my cloak and wept for my misfortune—not for his, but for my own, to think what a friend I had lost."

With the death of Socrates, the light of the Good was passed on to Plato, who was in many ways very different from his teacher. The most obvious was that he did write down Socrates' teachings, although even he retains some of his master's distrust for writing. Perhaps for this reason, in 387, he also founded a school, on a plot of land a mile north of Athens called "Hekedemia." There's not much to look at now. At the time, though, it consisted of a grove of olive trees sacred to Athena, whence we get our phrase "the groves of academe." In a way it was the world's first university, although there were not courses of study as we know them now. The goal was to transmit knowledge of the Good through that "flame that leapt from one soul to another." With the founding of the Academy, Plato had assured that the teaching of the Ideal would continue, and in the face-to-face method that Socrates would have preferred. Although the idea of a school was not new--the followers of Pythagoras had established communal organizations devoted to his teachings in the 6th BC century--Plato's Academy put it on a more formal footing. Although not much is known about its size or curriculum, it continued with a direct line of succession until 83BC, and was revived in 410 AD.

Other schools of "Postsocratics" also sprang up, challenging the establishment religion, including some whose names are still familiar today: Cynics, Stoics, Skeptics, Epicureans, Aristotelians. Looking back at them from our modern vantage point, we need to be reminded that they were not originally philosophies that could be neatly classified and discussed; rather their initial emphasis was in training the mind and the emotions into achieving a state of calm, ecstasy even, which comes from seeing through the transient appearances of the world. As Pierre

Hadot says in his excellent *Philosophy as a Way of Life*[2]:

> In their view, philosophy did not consist of teaching an abstract theory—much less in the exegesis of texts—but rather in the art of living. It is a concrete attitude and determinate lifestyle, which engages the whole of existence. The philosophical act is not situated merely on the cognitive level, but on that of the self and of being. It is a progress which causes us to be more fully, and makes us better. It is a conversion which turns our entire life upside down, changing the life of the person who goes through it. It raises the individual from an inauthentic condition of life, darkened by unconsciousness and harassed by worry, to an authentic state of life, in which he attains self-consciousness, an exact vision of the world, inner peace, and freedom.

Although this is not the place for a comprehensive account of these other schools[3], it is worth mentioning a few to show their diversity of approach. The Cynics,[4] who have come to mean people who are jaded and disillusioned, were not really a philosophical school at all but rather a kind of spontaneous movement whose common thread was a rejection of the establishment religion and social conventions. Think hippies in the 60's. For some this consisted of shocking the middle class by performing sex acts in public; for others it just meant living on the edge of society, homeless and without possessions, mental or otherwise. The archetypal cynic is Diogenes, a near-contemporary (and gadfly) to Plato. (He was described by Plato as "Socrates gone mad.") Diogenes believed himself to be more in the spirit of Socrates, like him being disdainful of wealth and reputation. Also like Socrates he wrote nothing, but did pass on his values (or lack of) to others by teaching and example.

By contrast Stoicism did involve a formal teaching and practices. It derives its name from the *Stoa,* shaded colonnades in the Agora at Athens where Zeno, its founder, would give lectures. The basic teaching was that a wise man does not allow his happiness to depend on external circumstances, and possesses a stillness and calm that allows him to be happy no matter what is happening "outside." He will receive pain and pleasure both with the same indifference. One of its most famous proponents was Epictetus, a slave who live around the first century AD, and was eventually freed and taught Stoicism to others. It was also a favorite philosophy for many Roman emperors, including Marcus Aurelius. While it is greatly concerned with ethics and just behavior, it does not seem to acknowledge anything beyond the individual as a source of the virtues it espouses.

By the time Plato died at his writing desk in about 348 BC at the age of 80, what is termed the "Golden Age" of Athens was long gone. With the help of some other subject-states, Athens had thrown off the yoke of the Spartans after the Peloponnesian War, and had regained its independence. It even established another mutual defense organization along the lines of the original Delian League. But it produced no leader with the charisma of Pericles, no monument as majestic as the Parthenon, and no clear heir to Socrates' Ideal. Ten years after Plato's death, Athens would be conquered by Phillip of Macedon, and would not regain its independence for another two thousand years.

But in another sense, a new kind of glory was just beginning. With the establishment of Plato's Academy and the rise of other philosophical schools, the influence of Greece as a cultural force took on new life. The star pupil of the Academy was Aristotle, about 40 years younger than Plato, who attended the academy from the age of about 18 until Plato's death. He was a man of catholic interests, although his focus was more on the things and workings of the world rather than the Good. But by becoming the personal tutor of Phillip's son Alexander, to be known as the Great, he insured that the Greek language and Greek learning would be carried East through what had been the Persian Empire and also into Egypt. Although Alexander never got to live there, he founded his namesake city, Alexandria, in Egypt, which eventually rivaled Athens as a center for learning. So, exceeding Pericles' description of Athens as "a school for Hellas," it had become a school to the world. What is usually called the Hellenistic world had begun.

After Philip was assassinated in 336, Alexander the Great took over the reins of the Macedonian army. So intent was he on conquering all the known world, he never really got to rule his vast empire. But his was the character of a conqueror, not a governor, and it is hard to imagine him settling down to rule. If his own army had not mutinied before his planned attack on

India, he may well have continued his brutal march all the way to the Pacific Ocean.

Alexander died in June of 323 BC at the age of thirty-two, under mysterious circumstances--a possible assassination by poisoning. After his death, his empire was divided up among his generals, and a period of relative peace followed. While local cultures were allowed to remain largely intact, the ruling classes spoke Greek, and it along with Greek learning became the standard for the empire. However, the learning that spread largely had the outward-looking influence of Aristotle. While the Academy of Plato continued in Athens, and similar esoteric schools flourished in Alexandria and other major cities, much of the literature and teaching during this period had a distinctly practical bent. The famous library at Alexandria was constructed and operated according to Aristotelian principles of classifying knowledge according to different subject areas, and had the mission of collecting copies of all known books, which at the time consisted of papyrus scrolls. It also supported a large population of scholars, and no doubt contained complete works of Plato, and possibly those of Pythagoras and Parmenides as well. Athens and other major cities also developed great libraries, although not on the scale of Alexandria's.

During this time, Athens and the rest of Greece, while nominally subjects of Macedonia, retained a fair amount of independence. Athens itself, as a major trading port, prospered, and maintained its tradition of intellectual inquiry. Many people from all over the world came to study at the Academy and to be initiated into the Mysteries at Eleusis.

The next major wave of conquest also came from the West in the form of Rome. Beginning in about 200 BC, the Romans began to exert their influence over Macedonia, largely through alliances and diplomacy, although always backed with the potential of military might. By about 150, Greece had become a subject state, although for practical purposes it had exchanged one set of rulers for another, and life went on pretty much as before. It is a cliché, but true, to say that while Rome conquered Greece, Greece actually conquered Rome, which adopted much of the Greek pantheon, mythology and literature. The Academy, however, did not fare so well, and closed in 83BC. Shortly thereafter, the Romans would also conquer Egypt, and with it Alexandria, in the process burning the famous library.

But like the Macedonians, the Romans were relatively hands-off rulers—they installed their own governors, but as long as the subject states paid their tribute, they were ruled with a light hand. The Greek language and cities continued to be the repositories for culture and things of the spirit. After the ministry of Jesus, for example, when St. Paul was working to establish Christian churches, he wrote in Greek largely to people in Greek cities: Corinth, Ephesus, Philippi.

The Romans were also an outward-oriented, practical people, and we do not know of any individuals during this time who was a clear heir to the Platonic tradition. Its influence though can be seen in the work of some scholars at the beginning of the current era. Plutarch was a native Greek, and a priest at the oracle of Delphi, who wrote on a wide variety of topics; it could be said that he originated the essay form. But while he demonstrates his knowledge of Plato, his concern is more with living a conventional virtuous life—he does not display a deep first-hand knowledge of the Ideal. Similarly, Philo (20 BC – 50 AD), born into a Jewish family in Alexandria, also displays a thorough understanding of "Platonism" and other schools of Greek thought, but quotes them primarily in support of Jewish doctrines.

By the third century, the Roman empire had reached its maximum size, covering the entire Mediterranean world and reaching further north to Britain, and what are now France and Germany. But because of its size and the rebellious natures of those at its borders, it had become ungovernable, resulting in what is usually called "the crisis of the third century"--a rapid turnover of emperors, and attendant political and military instability. The legitimate emperor during most of the period we will be looking at next, was Gallienus (c. 218 – 268AD), son of Valerian, who was forced to spend most of his reign putting out fires--attacks on the empire, as well as the division of the empire for a time into three separate parts. (He would ultimately meet the fate of many emperors during that century: assassination by his own soldiers.) But to most in the empire, these were distant problems, and unaware that the empire had begun its long slow decline, their lives went on pretty much as usual.

[1] Plato, *Phaedo*, trans. by Benjamin Jowett

[2] Pierre Hadot, *Philosophy as a Way of Life,* Blackwell Publishing, 1995

[3] For this, see Pierre Hadot's excellent *What is Ancient Philosophy?,* Harvard University, 2002

[4] In Ancient Greek, pronounced with a hard "c," and related to the word for "canine."

Chapter VI: Plotinus

Plotinus, 204/5-270

Plotinus (ca. AD 204/5–270), was born in Egypt, although his ancestry is not known. Little is actually known of his life, and this was according to his wish. His student Porphyry[1] begins his biography of him by saying, "Plotinus, the philosopher, our contemporary, seemed ashamed of being in the body. So deeply rooted was this feeling that he could never be induced to tell of his ancestry, his parentage, or his birthplace." It is generally acknowledged though that he came to Alexandria at the age of about 27 in order to study philosophy, but could not find any teacher who inspired him. At the suggestion of a friend, he finally went to hear one Ammonius, of whom also little is known, and declared "This was the man I was looking for." He stayed in Alexandria and studied with him for 11 years. After an ill-fated attempt to learn more of the teachings of Persia and India, he went to Rome at the age of forty and established his own circle of followers. (The emperor Gallienus[2], while perhaps not part of the circle, did know Plotinus, and seemed to be sympathetic to his teaching. At one point Plotinus petitioned him for a plot of land on which to build a Platonic city, but the senate, with which Gallienus had bad relations, turned it down.)

Almost all that we know of Plotinus comes from Porphyry, who was to him pretty much what Plato was to Socrates. Although Plotinus was not averse to writing down his teaching, he did so with little regard to grammar, spelling or continuity, and Porphyry provided those editorial services. According to Porphyry, "He used to work out his design mentally from first to last; when he came to set down his ideas, he wrote at one jet all that he had stored in his mind as though he were copying from a book."

Porphyry arranged Plotinus' works into six books of nine essays; hence Enneads. It is sometime hard to believe they were written by the same person, since their tone can range from inspired poetry to hair-splitting pedantry. But he is consistent in his inconsistency; with no regard for himself or how he appeared, he seems to have been most set on being true to the source of the words. In the same biography, Porphyry says: "Interrupted, perhaps, by someone entering on business, he never lost hold of his plan; he was able to meet all the demands of the conversation and still keep his own train of thought clearly before him; when he was free again, he never looked over what he had previously written--his sight, it has been mentioned, did not allow of such rereading--but he linked on what was to follow as if no distraction had occurred."

For someone who provided one of the West's enduring mystical masterpieces, Plotinus seems to have been remarkably down-to-earth. Porphyry tells us that often his students, "on the approach of death," had turned over their children and property to his care, and that "He always found time for those that came to submit returns of the children's property, and he looked closely to the accuracy of the accounts: 'Until the young people take to philosophy,' he use to say, 'their fortunes and revenues must be kept intact for them.' And yet all this labour and thought over the worldly interests of so many people never interrupted, during waking hours, his intention towards the Supreme." He goes on to describe him as "Good and kindly, singularly gentle and engaging..., sleeplessly alert..., pure of soul, ever striving towards the divine which he loved with all his being...."

"The One" is Plotinus' word for this divine, the Ideal, and he never loses sight of it, even when splitting the finest of hairs. As Elmer O'Brien, S.J. says in his enlightening introduction to him, "Anyone who would succeed in understanding Plotinus must seat himself squarely before the concept of The One."[3] And so it is to that which we turn our attention next.

When he speaks of The One (*to Hen*), we see both sides of Plotinus: the poet as well as the pedant. As pedant, he appeals to the mind while at the same time trying to show the mind's inadequacy to understand it, much as Socrates did with Glaucon. He realizes the fruitlessness of words to describe it, yet try he must.

> Its definition, in fact, could be only 'the indefinable': what is not a thing is not some definite thing. We are in agony for a true expression; we are talking of the untellable; we name, only to indicate for our own use as best we may. And this name, The One, contains really no more that the negation of plurality; under the same pressure the Pythagoreans found their indication in the symbol 'Apollo' ("Αpollon," a=not, pollon=many) with its repudiation of the multiple. If we are led to think positively of The One, name and thing, there would be more truth in silence...."4

(An interesting revelation about Apollo, the sun god, given what we have learned from Socrates about "the child of The Good.")

Plotinus tries to describe the same unity central to the Indian philosophy of *advaita*--"not two." What he is proposing is not even monotheism, since to say "One God" creates a supreme being "out there," which is separate from us. So like the Zen master with a koan, he tries to short-circuit the discursive mind and perhaps allow the One to appear.

But I certainly don't mean to denigrate his intellectual rigor in insisting on The One being not less than "the untellable." In his time, and throughout history, much evil was perpetrated by people who took The One to be less; who limited the limitless and created it in their own image. The whole sad history of ethnic and religious conflict is the result of claiming myself to be chosen by the One, and then seeing everyone else as lesser than I am. Plotinus explicitly warns against identifying with this duality "The One is absent from nothing and from everything. It is present only to those who are prepared for it and are able to receive it, to enter into harmony with it, to grasp and to touch it by virtue of their likeness to it, by virtue of that inner power similar to and stemming from The One when it is in that state in which it was when it originated from The One."5 The One is one; there is no "other."

And Plotinus is very clear that this unity can be known. In *The Descent of the Soul* he says: "It has happened often. Roused into myself from my body-- outside everything else and inside myself--my gaze has met a beauty wondrous and great. At such moments I have been certain that mine was the better part, mine the best of lives lived to the fullest, mine identity with the divine. Fixed there firmly, poised above everything in the intellectual that is less than the highest, utter actuality was mine." 6

How could it be that in that state we would wish anyone harm? How could we see anyone else as "other?" Listen further:

> The chief difficulty is this: awareness of The One comes to us neither by knowing nor by the pure thought that discovers the other intelligible things, but by a presence transcending knowledge. When the soul knows something, it loses its unity, it cannot remain simply one because knowledge implies multiplicity. The soul

then misses The One and falls into number and multiplicity.

Therefore we must go beyond knowledge and hold to unity. We must renounce knowing and knowable, every object of thought, even Beauty, because Beauty, too, is posterior to The One and is derived from it as, from the sun, the daylight. That is why Plato says of The One, 'It can neither be spoken of nor written about.' If nevertheless we speak of it and write about it, we do so only to give direction, to urge towards that vision beyond discourse, to point out the road to one desirous of seeing.7

As The One does not contain any difference, it is always present and we are present to it when we no longer contain difference. The One does not aspire to us, to move around us; we aspire to it, to move around it. Actually, we always move around it; but we do not always look. We are like a chorus grouped around a conductor who allow their attention to be distracted by the audience. If, however, they were to turn towards their conductor, they would sing as they should and would really be with him. We are always around The One. If we were not, we would dissolve and cease to exist. Yet our gaze does not remain fixed upon The One. When we look at it, we then attain the end of our desires and find rest. Then it is that, all discord past, we dance an inspired dance around it.

In this dance the soul looks upon the source of life, the source of The Intelligence, the origin of Being, the cause of the Good, the root of the Soul.8

Here we are obviously hearing Plotinus the poet, in a rapturous state of inspiration, and the ease with which he changes to that from the teacher is evidence that he did not think of himself as one or the other. He is a model for the renunciation of all labels, all the adjectives--even the flattering ones--with which we limit ourselves. I am a male; no, I am The One. I am intelligent; no, I am The Intelligence. I am unloved; no, I am Love.

Now of course Plotinus does go on to construct a very elaborate cosmology in works such as "*The Origin and Order of the Beings following on the First.*" But it is rather absurd of us to try to analyze this cosmology without some first-hand experience of it. His aim, I think, is to show to us just how vast is this universe within us; let us just open our eyes to the next larger circle and get a glimpse of the unity toward which it all tends. Then we can analyze if we must, but more likely we will realize that

> We are not separated from The One, not distant from it, even though bodily nature has closed about us and drawn us to itself. It is because of The One that we breathe and have our being: it does not bestow its gifts at one moment only to leave us again; its giving is without cessation so long as it remains what it is. As we turn towards The One, we exist to a higher degree, while to withdraw from it is to fall. Our soul is delivered from evil by rising to that place which is free of all evils. There it knows. There it is immune. There it truly lives.

Life not united with the divinity is shadow
and mimicry of authentic life. Life there is
the native act of The Intelligence, which,
motionless in its contact with The One,
gives birth to gods, beauty, justice, and
virtue.9

Although his descriptions are different, Plotinus
is as clear as was Plato in the assertion that The One,
of the Ideal, is our true state. As with the prisoners in
the cave, we spend our lives in a state of "shadow and
mimicry of authentic life," while all the while "we are
not separated from The One." And while Plotinus does
spend time talking about how we come to this state of
shadow (*The Descent of the Soul*), his main concern is
in helping us return to the authentic life.

The means that Plotinus prescribes for attaining
this return, in addition to dialectic, is contemplation.
This is a translation of the Greek *theoria* (θεωρία)
with its roots both in "seeing" and "god," and which in
English has unfortunately taken on the meaning of
"thinking about." Plotinus describes it quite fully in
Ennead III, *On Contemplation*, the study of which this
chapter is no substitute. Elmer O'Brien says of it,
"This treatise is, perhaps, the best single instance of
the mature thought and method of Plotinus. It repays
an attentive reading." Its conclusion can give us
insight as well as motivation:

The Intelligence is beautiful--of all things the
most beautiful. Dwelling in pure light and
"stainless radiance," it envelops everything with
its own light. The realm of sense, so beautiful, is
only its reflected shadow. It abides in full
resplendence because it contains nothing dark to

the mind or obscure or indefinite. It knows beatitude.

Wonder seizes upon him who contemplates it, who enters in and becomes one with it. Just as the view of the heavens and the splendor of the stars leads one to think of their author and to see him out, so the contemplative who has gazed upon the intelligible realm and been struck with the wonder of it should seek out its author-- should ask who has given it existence, where the author is, and how he authored it.

From whom comes such beauty as this, this procession of plentitude? Not the Intelligence, nor Being, but their prior. They come after it because they have need of both thought and fulfillment. But they are close to that which wants for nothing, which need not even think.

So high is its rank, The Intelligence is authentic plentitude and thought. Its prior is neither for if it were, it would not be what it is--the Good.[10]

For the rest of this chapter, I will dispense with the commentary and just present Plotinus himself, where he is, as he is--but whose writing, I might only add, is not Strunked and Whitened. It requires, but rewards, sustained attention.

Happiness

If, then, the perfect life is within human reach, the man attaining it attains happiness: if not, happiness must be made over to the gods, for the perfect life is for them alone.

But since we hold that happiness is for human beings too, we must consider what this perfect life is. The matter may be stated thus:

It has been shown elsewhere that man when he commands not merely the life of sensation but also Reason and Authentic Intellection, has realized the perfect life.

But are we to picture this kind of life as something foreign imported into his nature?

No: there exists no single human being that does not either potentially or effectively possess this thing which we hold to constitute happiness.

But are we to think of man as including this form of life, the perfect, after the manner of a partial constituent of his entire nature?

We say, rather, that while in some men it is present as a mere portion of their total being--in those, namely, that have it potentially--there is, too, the man, already in possession of true felicity, who is this perfection realized, who has passed over into actual identification with it. All else is now mere clothing about the man, not to be called part of him since it lies about him unsought, not his because not appropriated to himself by any act of the will.

To the man in this state, what is the Good?

He himself by what he has and is.

And the author and principle of what he is and holds is the Supreme, which within Itself is the Good but manifests Itself within the human being after this other mode.

The sign that this state has been achieved is that the man seeks nothing else.

What indeed could he be seeking? Certainly none of the less worthy things; and the Best he carries always within him.

He that has such a life as this has all he needs in life.

Once the man is a Proficient, the means of happiness, the way to the good, are within, for nothing is good that lies outside him. Anything he desires further than this he seeks as a necessity, and not for himself but for a subordinate, for the body bound to him, to which since it has life he must minister the needs of life, not needs, however, to the true man of this degree. He knows himself to stand above all such things, and what he gives to the lower he so gives as to leave his true life undiminished.

Adverse fortune does not shake his felicity: the life so founded is stable ever. Suppose death strikes at his household or at his friends; he knows what death is, as the victims, if they are among the wise, know too. And if death taking from him his familiars and intimates does bring grief, it is not to him, not to the true man, but to that in him which stands apart from the Supreme, to that lower man in whose distress he takes no part.(I, 4, 4)

Beauty

Chiefly beauty is visual. Yet in word patterns and in music (for cadences and rhythms are beautiful) it addresses itself to the hearing as well. Dedicated living, achievement, character, intellectual pursuits are beautiful to those who rise above the realm of the senses; to such ones the virtues, too, are beautiful. Whether the range of beauty goes beyond these will become clear in the course of this exposition....

It is impossible to talk about bodily beauty if one, like one born blind, has never seen and known bodily beauty. In the same way, it is impossible to talk about the "luster" of right living and of learning and of the like if one has never cared for such things, never beheld "the face of justice" and temperance and seen it to be "beyond the beauty of evening or morning star." Seeing of this sort is done only with the eye of the soul. And, seeing thus, one undergoes a joy, a wonder, and a distress more deep than any other because here one touches truth.....

What is this vision like? How is it attained? How will one see this immense beauty that dwells, as it were, in inner sanctuaries and comes not forward to be seen by the profane? Let him who can arise, withdraw into himself, forgo all that is known by the eyes, turn aside from the bodily beauty that was once his joy. He must not hanker after the graceful shapes that appear in bodies, but know them for copies, for traceries, for shadows, and hasten away towards that which they bespeak. ....We must close our eyes and invoke a new manner of seeing, a wakefulness that is the birthright of us all, though few put it to use.

What, then, is this inner vision?

Like anyone just awakened, the soul cannot look at bright objects. It must be persuaded to look first at beautiful habits, then the works of beauty produced not by craftsman's skill but by the virtue of men known for their goodness, then the souls of those who achieve beautiful deeds. "How can one see the beauty of a good soul?" Withdraw into yourself and look. If you do not as yet see beauty within you, do as does the sculptor of a statue that is to be beautified: he cuts away here, he smooths it there, he makes this line lighter, this one purer, until he disengages beautiful lineaments in the marble. Do you this, too. Cut away all that is excessive, straighten all that is crooked, bring light to all that is overcast, labor to make all one radiance of beauty. Never cease "working at the statue" until there shines out upon you from it the divine sheen of virtue, until you see perfect "goodness firmly established in the stainless shrine."

....No eye that has not become like unto the sun will ever look upon the sun; nor will any that is not beautiful look upon the beautiful. Let each one therefore become godlike and beautiful who would contemplate the divine and beautiful. (I, 6, 1-9)

Love

Does each individual Soul, then, contain within itself such a Love in essence and substantial reality?

Since not only the pure All-soul but also that of the Universe contains such a Love, it would be difficult to explain why our personal soul should not. It must be so, even, with all that has life.

This indwelling love is not other than the Spirit which, as we are told, walks with every being, the affection dominant in each several nature. It implants the characteristic desire; the particular Soul, strained towards its own natural objects, brings forth its own Eros, the guiding spirit realizing its worth and the quality of its Being.

As the All-soul contains the Universal Love, so must the single soul be allowed its own single Love: and as closely as the single Soul holds to the All-Soul, never cut off but embraced within it, the two together constituting one principle of life, so the single separate Love holds to the All-Love. (III, 5, 4)

Every soul is an Aphrodite, as is suggested in the myth of Aphrodite's birth at the same time as that of Eros. As long as soul stays true to itself, it loves the divinity and desires to be one with it, as a daughter loves with a noble love a noble father.

When, however, the soul has come down here to human birth, it exchanges (as if deceived by the false promises of an adulterous lover) its divine love for one that is mortal. And then, far from its begetter, the soul yields to all manner of excess.

But, when the soul begins to hate its shame and puts away evil and makes its return, it finds peace.

How great, then, is its bliss can be conceived by those who have not tasted it if they but think of earthly unions in love, marking well the joy felt by the lover who succeeds in obtaining his desires. But this love is directed to the mortal and harmful--to shadows--and soon disappears because such is not the authentic object of our love nor the good we really seek. Only in the world beyond does the real object of our love exist, the only one with which we can unite ourselves, of which we can have a part and which we can intimately possess without being separated by the barriers of flesh.

Anyone who has had this experience will know what I am talking about. He will know that the soul lives another life as it advances towards the One, reaches it and shares in it. Thus restored, the soul recognizes the presence of the dispenser of the true life. It needs nothing more. On the contrary, it must renounce everything else and rest in it alone, become it alone, all earthiness gone, eager to be free, impatient of every fetter that binds below in order so to embrace the real object of its love with its entire being that no part of it does not touch the One. (VI, 9, 9)

[1]Porphyry: *On the Life of Plotinus and His Work.* Reprinted in *The Enneads: Abridged Edition,* translated by Stephen McKenna, Penguin Books, 1991

[2]For more on Rome in the 3d century (all centuries, actually), subscribe to *The History of Rome,* a podcast by Mike Duncan. In particular, episodes 111-116 deal with this era, and provide a balanced portrait of Gallienus. As with most histories though it is mostly kings and generals: no mention of Plotinus.

[3]Plotinus, *The Essential Plotinus: Representative Treatises from the Enneads,* translated by Elmer O'Brien, S.J. Hackett Publishing, 1964, p. 18

[4]Plotinus, *The Enneads,* translated by Stephen McKenna, Penguin Books, 1991, p. 398

[5]Plotinus, *The Essential Plotinus: Representative Treatises from the Enneads,* translated by Elmer O'Brien, S.J. Hackett Publishing, 1964, p. 79. (When possible, I use O'Brien's translation; I generally find it clearer, but with the ability to soar when its author does.)

[6]Ibid., p. 62

[7]Ibid., p. 78

[8]Ibid., p. 84

[8]Ibid., p. 85

[10]Ibid., p. 175

Chapter VII: Forgetting the Ideal

Plotinus died in 270 at the age of 66; according to Eustochius, a student who was present, his last words were, "I am striving to give back the Divine in myself to the Divine in the All." Due to his ill-health, he had retired to a country house some time before, and his circle had diminished. Porphyry, his biographer and editor, went on to publish Plotinus' works, and to become a carrier of the torch of the Ideal himself, although his light did not shine as brightly. But like Plotinus, he realized that union with the Divine was available to humans; in fact he says, "To this God, I also declare, I Porphyry, that in my sixty-eighth year I too was once admitted and entered into Union." What came to be known as "Neoplatonism" was given a new life through his work, both in Rome and other parts of the empire.

The empire itself, which had been divided into three parts for most of the century, was reunited under the emperor Diocletian. But eventually he had to admit that the size of the empire and the number of attacks and revolts that had become commonplace made it ungovernable. In the late 3d century he deliberately divided the empire into Eastern and Western, each ruled by a senior and junior "Augustus." This system proved workable for a while, and a period of relative calm ensued. Rome itself however declined in influence as the seat of power moved north to around Milan in the Western Empire, and Byzantium in the Eastern.

Just as the emperors during this period were not for the most part native to the Italian peninsula, the "successors" to Plato and Plotinus also came from far-flung parts of the empire. Porphyry himself (this, like "Plato" was also a nickname, derived from the Greek word for "purple," denoting royalty) had been born in Tyre, in what is now the southern part of Lebanon, and had come to Rome after studying at the Academy in Athens. Late in his life he married a woman named Marcella, and his letter to her exhorting to the study of philosophy still stands as one of his most popular works. "As there is no profit in the physician's art unless it cure the diseases of the body, so there is none in philosophy, unless it expel the troubles of the soul."[1] On Plotinus' death, Porphyry took over as the successor, and he too attracted many students.

One of the most famous of these (although it is not certain he was a direct student) was Iamblichus, who, like Porphyry, was born in what is now Syria or Lebanon. After studying in Rome, he returned to Syria around 304 and founded his own school. Although most of his original writing have been lost, much of his teaching has been preserved in the work of his students, and it consists for the most part of elaborations of the Plotinian hierarchy, the source of which was of course The One.

Equally famous was Proclus, who was born also in the Eastern Empire--Constantinople--in 412. He received most of his philosophical training in Alexandria, and then moved to Athens where he eventually became head of the Academy. Because of this, and because of his devotion to the works of Plato, he is often called "The Successor." He wrote commentaries on a number of works by Plato as well as other philosophical systems. Like Plotinus, he is capable of extremely dense discursive reasoning, alternating with moments of poetic beauty. In his *Commentary on the Chaldean Oracles,* he says, "Let us not therefore imagine that we may persuade the Master of true discourses by a strange hurricane of words, nor by show or parade adorned with artificial rites: for God loves the simple, unadorned beauty of form."[2] Unfortunately, what follows after is one of the most incomprehensible "hurricane of words" in the neo-Platonic literature. Notwithstanding, his influence on other philosophers of the Middle Ages and beyond has been great.[3]

But of course the real force weighing on "Idealism" around this time, and increasingly during the 5th century was Christianity. The Emperor Constantine (272-37) had been the first to convert to Christianity and in 311, with the Edict of Milan, had reversed the empire-wide practice of persecuting Christians. (Actually it was a blanket recognition of religious tolerance in which Christians were included--quite visionary.) It was declared the state religion in 380 under the authority of the Pope, based in Rome.

Christianity and Platonism had for many years maintained a kind of peaceful coexistence, and in fact many of the early churchmen were articulate Platonists as well. St. Augustine (354-430) was a practicing Platonist before joining the church, and his writing remained full of Platonic ideas. In fact, during the Middle Ages, when many of Plato's original manuscripts were lost, Augustine's writings were a major source of knowledge about the Ideal.

But the evangelistic spirit of Christianity and its requirement that converts had to renounce all other religions brought it into conflict with Platonism. While some churchmen continued to consider Plato's teaching almost on the same level as that of Jesus, officially they became considered pagan along with other forms of philosophy and Greco-Roman polytheism. In 391, at the order of the Emperor Theodosius, paganism was declared illegal, and the patriarch of Alexandria, Theophilus, used the occasion to order the destruction of the famous library. In 415, in one of history's many tragic reversals where those persecuted become the persecutors, the Platonic philosopher and mathematician Hypatia was brutally murdered by a mob of Christians. Her death had a chilling effect on the teaching of Plato from which the Alexandrian schools would not recover.

The Empire, in particular the Western, had continued a long, slow decline. The rift between East and West had grown, and the turnover of Emperors returned to levels seen during the Crisis of the Third Century. The year 476 is generally given as the "fall" of Rome, when the Gothic invaders deposed the last nominal Emperor, Romulus Augustus. But in fact the empire had already become a pale shadow of its former self, and a confluence of church and state now came together as a new form of governance. The church became a political force as well, with its own territories and its own army.

Boethius, born shortly after the "fall," grew up under the influence of both Christianity and Platonism, and seemed to see no conflict between the two. He rose to a high position of authority under the rule of King Theodoric "the Great," and had planned a project to translate all Plato's dialogs into Latin. But Theodoric came to believe that Boethius was conspiring against him with the Eastern Empire, and ordered him executed in 525. While in prison, Boethius wrote the classic *Consolation of Philosophy,* which is Platonic through and through in form (a dialog between the author and the goddess Philosophy) and content (there is one Good, which is the source of all we can know or see).

> The goddess: ...it is plain that the essence of the good and of happiness is one and the same."
>
> "I cannot see how any one can think otherwise."
>
> "But we have shewn that God and true happiness are one and the same."
>
> "Yes."
>
> "Therefore," said she, "we may safely conclude that the essence of God also lies in the absolute good and nowhere else."[4]

The translation project was likely never started.

Just four years later, in 529, the Eastern Emperor Justinian ordered the closing of all pagan schools, including the Academy in Athens, and the Western World entered into a period of sleep from which it would not emerge for another 900 years.

[1]Porphyry, *Letter to Marcella,* in Algis Uzdavinys, ed., *The Golden Chain.* World Wisdom, 2004

2Proclus, *Commentary on the Chaldean Oracles,* in Algis Uzdavinys, ed., op. cit.

3Ralph Waldo Emerson, in a journal entry in 1842 says,

I read Proclus for my opium ; it excites my imagination to let sail before me the pleasing and grand figures of gods and daemons and demoniacal men. I hear of rumors rife among the most ancient gods, of azonic gods who are itinerants, of daemons with fulgid eyes, of the unenvying and exuberant will of the gods ; the aquatic gods, the Plain of Truth, the meadow, the nutriment of the gods, the paternal port, and all the rest of the Platonic rhetoric quoted as household words. By all these and so many rare and brave words I am filled with hilarity and spring, my heart dances, my sight is quickened, I behold shining relations between all beings, and am impelled to write and almost to sing. I think one would grow handsome who read Proclus much and well.

(When I read Proclus, my eyes glaze over and I want to take a nap. But that's why Emerson is Emerson, and I'll never be very good-looking.)

4A number of translations are available online, such as those at the Internet Archive,

http://www.archive.org/

Chapter VIII: The Florentine Renaissance

Ah, the Renaissance! Ah, Florence! Along with Classical Athens, one of the most romanticized times and places in history. Don't expect to find a comprehensive history of the period here--there are any number of fine accounts available beginning with Jacob Burkhardt's *The Civilization of the Renaissance in Italy*, and they make for fascinating reading (and viewing--the explosion in the visual arts is the feature still most associated with the Renaissance). We will be concentrating here on the events most relevant to the "rebirth" of the knowledge of the Ideal.

But first: what is this Renaissance thing anyway? It has over the years become a catchall term applied to a number of different artistic movements and activities that began in about the 14th century and continued through the 16th. It was to a large extent a reaction against the frozen and rigid religious and social systems of the Middle Ages, exemplified by the stony, expressionless statues of saints found in medieval cathedrals. In broad terms, it had to do with the rediscovery of ancient art forms and schools of thought, but it also carried with it an implicit empowerment of human beings, including the possibility of becoming godlike themselves.

Weren't these frozen statues and social systems exemplars of Plato's eternal and unchanging forms? Wouldn't he have approved of the power of the church/state to limit the access of people to "bad" influences and encourage them to concentrate on the unseen world of "spirit?" Well, of course I can't pretend to speak for Plato, but my own feeling is that I think not. The church at this time had become extremely self-serving, determined to increase its own power by using fear and intimidation as tools. One need only look at a typical painting of the Middle Ages showing the torments of the sinners down in Hell, contrasted with the positioning of the churchmen and saints to get the not-so-subtle message that devotion to the church was the only way to escape eternal suffering. So I think that Plato (as well as Plotinus), who believed that each human carried the spark of the divine, would have railed against this view that access to the godlike nature is open only to a few.

Back to the events at hand. Despite being 2000 years apart, there are a number of similarities between this age and Plato's. As mentioned before, Italy was strewn throughout with reminders of "the glory that was Rome," in the form of ruins, sculptures, roads, aqueducts, stadiums, as well as the Latin language itself, which was still used for scholarly (read church) and legal writing. As Italy at this time began to wake up to the significance of its past, it also began to realize that it was capable of recreating this glory.

Also as in ancient Greece, Italy was divided into a number of city-states, and most were ruled by an oligarchy of old and powerful families. The papacy also controlled its own lands, which comprised a large swath of central and northern Italy, as well as its own army. Florence was actually the most democratic, with some provision for representation by the various trade guilds--weavers, dyers, and others in the textile industry, which was the basis of the Florentine economy. As with Greece, there was almost constant conflict among the city-states, with shifting political alliances, as well as within them, with Montague-and-Capulet-worthy street fights among different families. Power was sought wherever it could be found, from arranged marriages to producing sons who could become highly placed in the Church hierarchy.

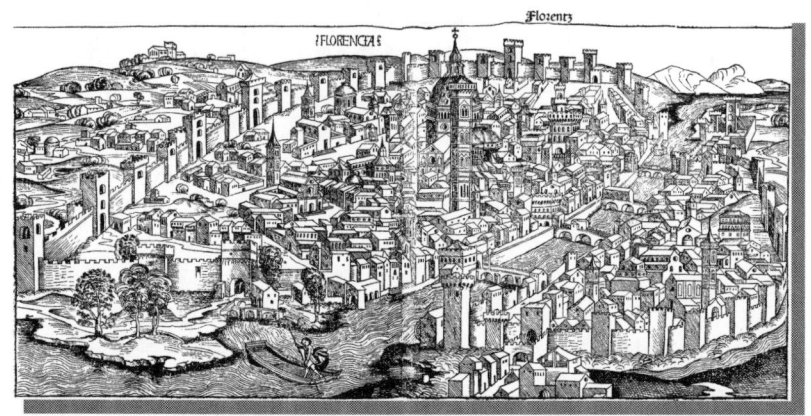

Woodcut of Florence, 1493

The family that would dominate Florentine politics and cultural life in the Renaissance was the Medici. Relatively *nouveau riche* by Florentine standards, they made their money through a vast international banking enterprise, which also helped make Florence's coinage, the florin, the de facto currency for all of Europe. The *Pater Patriae* was Cosimo de Medici whose influence touched everything that happened in Florence from 1434, when he returned from a year's exile in Venice, until his death in 1464. Personally unassuming--he often walked the streets of Florence without a bodyguard--he nonetheless used his great wealth to support many civic and artistic projects that would assure his role in history. Not the least of these was his financing of the famous dome created by Brunelleschi on the Basilica of Santa Maria del Fiore, which was to Florence what the Parthenon was to Athens.

Cosimo also had a natural affinity for philosophy, and used his agents in European capitals to help rediscover philosophical texts that had been lost since the fall of the Empire. One can only imagine the wonder and excitement that reading these manuscripts must have engendered. In addition to long-forgotten books retrieved from monasteries, Cosimo also obtained many from parts of the Eastern Empire which had been preserved by Islamic and Jewish scholars. Among these were works of Hermes Trismagistus, believed at this time to have been an ancient figure who gave his wisdom to both Eastern and Western traditions.

The real coup of Cosimo's collecting began in the year 1439 when he agreed to sponsor the church's council which was charged with seeking to reunite the Western and Eastern churches. This council had been meeting in Basel and then in Ferrara when Cosimo agreed to sponsor it (and also allow its participants to escape the plague which was afflicting Ferrara). Although it ultimately failed to repair the schism, it did reintroduce to the West a more complete corpus of the works of Plato than had been available. In attendance was a representative of the Greek Orthodox church named Georgius Gemistus, later also known by the nickname Pletho, who brought many Platonic dialogs in Greek, and who also gave lectures on "Idealism" to Cosimo and other Florentine intellectuals. Such was the effect of these lectures that they gave him the title of "the second Plato," and established their own *Accademmia Platonica*. The task of translating the manuscripts from the Greek was given to the young Marsilio Ficino, about whom much more later.

It would be satisfying to say that once Plato was reintroduced to the West, his inspiration ushered in a new age of creativity and devotion to the Ideal. In fact, the artistic achievements which we associate with the Renaissance were well under way, but the Accademmia did give inspiration to a new generation of artists--among them Michelangelo, Raphael, and Botticelli[1]--as well as a new visual vocabulary which included Greek gods and myths. Raphael, although born in Urbino, spent a number of years in Florence, and his study of Plato and his philosophical lineage is evident in the painting "The School of Athens."

Lorenzo de Medici,
after Verrocchio, 1480

Cosimo died in 1464, and his responsibilities passed to his son Piero, who had an advanced case of gout and did not live long. His premature death in 1469 passed the leadership of Florence to his son Lorenzo, to be known as The Magnificent, when Lorenzo was only twenty. He had lived a privileged and self-indulgent life, but when the call came he answered it with great dedication. Although he did not have Cosimo's business sense (and the bank suffered during his tenure), his diplomatic skills saw the republic through a number of crises during his lifetime. The most extreme of these was the Pazzi conspiracy, orchestrated by the Florentine family of that name with the complicity of Pope Sixtus IV, which attempted to murder Lorenzo during high mass at the Cathedral, and did in fact kill his younger brother Giuliano. Sixtus was eager to conquer Florence to add to his own power, and when the assassination failed, he entered into war with Florence for a number of years.

The end of the 15th century saw a rise in religious fundamentalism embodied in the person of Girolamo Savonarola, a Dominican friar who condemned what he saw as the immorality of much of the art being produced, and the luxuriousness of the lifestyles of the rich Florentines. He was also a severe critic of the corruption in the church, castigating Medici and popes alike. He espoused an austere way of life and is famous (or infamous) for promoting the "bonfire of the vanities," at which citizens would bring (or have brought for them) worldly possession such as books, paintings, clothing, furniture or anything else deemed to be immoral. Ostensibly the priest for the Medici family, it is said that he refused last rites to Lorenzo when he died in 1492.

Savonarola managed to use the presence of various natural calamities in Florence as evidence that its citizens were being punished by God for their worldliness. He counted among his followers the former humanists Pico della Mirandola and Sandro Botticelli, who burned a number of his own paintings on the bonfires. When the promised relief from plagues and famine did not materialize, the city turned against Savonarola. In 1498 he was excommunicated by Pope Alexander VI, and after weeks of torture, he was burned to death in the Piazza della Signoria.

But Florence would not recover its prior glory. Savonarola had exiled the Medici and their prize artist Michelangelo, who would go to Rome and produce his most famous works. While the influence of the Ideal was not forgotten as completely as it was in the millennium before, it did recede into the background and into the universities as the religious conflicts of the Reformation broke out. In the next chapter we will see how it burned brightly in the lives of two adopted Florentines, Pico della Mirandola and especially Marsilio Ficino.

[1]Of Sandro Botticelli, Maurice Rowdon says, "Like Pico della Mirandola and Marsilio Ficino he was looking for a certain enchanted stillness, the food of all religious experience, the common principle of all theologies." Maurice Rowdon, *Lorenzo the Magnificent,* Henry Regnery, 1974

Chapter IX: Pico and Ficino

The Renaissance is best known for its artistic and architectural achievements; for the names of Leonardo, Michelangelo, Brunelleschi, Raphael, Botticelli and many others. But it was the rediscovery of Platonic and other early texts that provided a philosophical underpinning for much of this work. It provided a new view of man, not as a creature damned by original sin which could only be expiated through the church, but as a rational being, full of wonders in his "natural" state, and one who could choose to reclaim his godlike status through the exercise of his reason. In this chapter, we will look at two of the most influential proponents of this view, Marsilio Ficino and Giovanni Pico della Mirandola.

Ficino was born in 1433, the year before Cosimo de Medici returned to Florence after an exile in Venice, and his life would be intertwined with the Medici for the rest of the century. Cosimo had been exiled by rival factions who feared his money was buying him too much power, and they were right-- when he left and took his money with him, the economic hardship became so great he was asked back. When he did return, he became the de facto ruler of Florence, and used his great wealth to support many civic projects, as well as artists and scholars. Ficino was one of these.

His father Diotifeci, ("God made thee") was Cosimo's personal physician, who nonetheless did not become wealthy himself because of his habit of not charging the poor who also came to him for care.

Marsilio was scholastically precocious, especially in the field of languages, and early on he was put to work by Cosimo editing and translating the many ancient texts that were being recovered throughout Europe. In addition to his skill with words, he was also an accomplished musician and healer.

Detail from "Zaccaria in the Temple" by Ghirlandaio, showing Ficino (left) and members of his Academy: Christoforo Landino, Angelo Poliziano, and Demetrios Chalkondyles

He also seems to have taken naturally to the scholarly and spiritual life, and to possess the constancy of purpose and habits that enabled his prodigious output of translation and writing. In a letter in 1476 he says to Carlo Valguli, "You ask me, my Valguli, what am I doing today? That which I did yesterday. Again you ask what am I planning to do tomorrow? That which I am doing today. Our Plato has persuaded me that I would in the end accomplish most if I always did the same thing."[1] He did not

marry or have a romantic relationship that is known--
his love, expressed throughout his writing, was
Platonic. In 1473, after a serious illness, he became a
priest of the Catholic church and a canon of the
Florence cathedral.

Like most Renaissance scholars, he pursued
studies in many different fields of learning being
rediscovered, among them astrology and "magic,"
which landed him in some trouble with the hierarchy
of the church, although not as much as Pico and some
others. Ficino knew how to phrase his thoughts so
they did not appear threatening to the church, and of
course he had the protection of the Medici. He became
tutor to Cosimo's grandson Lorenzo, who would
continue to support Ficino's work when he came into
power.

When Ficino was thirty, Cosimo assigned him to
what would be his greatest achievement: the
translation of all the newly rediscovered Platonic
dialogs from Greek into Latin, realizing the plan of
Boethius from 900 years before. And as mentioned in
the previous chapter, he interrupted this work
partway through to translate the works of Hermes
Trismegistus which had recently been brought from
Constantinople, and afterward translated many of the
neo-Platonists also, Plotinus and Proclus among
them. In addition to the translations though, he
produced many of his own works, and it soon becomes
evident when reading any of them that he is not just
refashioning ancients texts; he has penetrated into the
good himself and is writing from first-hand
experience.

For example, in a late essay *The Book of the Sun (De Sole)* he invokes Plato's analogy of the sun as "the child of the Good," and says:

> Seeing that it really is possible to ascend to the archetypal pattern partly by the taking away of that which is worse and partly by the adding of what is better, take from the Sun - from whom Averroes took gross physical matter - all definite quantity. But leave it with the potency of light, so that there will remain the light itself, cleansed by miraculous power, defined neither by a definite quantity nor by any definite shape, filling with its presence a space immense with respect to the imagination. This pure light exceeds the intelligence just as in itself sunlight surpasses the acuity of the eyes. In this way, in proportion to the strength you receive from the Sun, you will almost seem to have found God, who placed his tabernacle in the Sun.[2]

As previously mentioned, Ficino's circle formed an *Accademmia Platonica,* which provided an intellectual background to many of the more visible activities of the quattrocentro. Peter Hall has put it:

> Marsilio Ficino's Platonic Academy played a particular role. It was not an organized institution like the academies of the sixteenth century, but merely a circle around Ficino. Its activities were closely linked with Ficino himself: improvised conversations with friends or visitors; organized banquets and discussions such as the famous celebrations on Plato's birthday; speeches or declamations delivered by Ficino; public courses given by Ficino in the church of

Santa Maria degli Angeli on Plato, on Plotinus, on St Paul; and some private instruction, based on reading Plato and perhaps other authors. It sought to bridge the yawning gap between medieval dogmatic theology and Aristotelian scholasticism, through a metaphysical Platonism based on reason.[3]

He used his unique position as a Platonist as well as a priest of the church to attempt a reconciliation between the two, as so many others had done before him. It is generally acknowledged that his articulation of the doctrine of "the immortality of the soul," as described by Plato in the Phaedo, caused it to become adopted by the church.[4]

Giovanni Pico della Mirandola would seem to be a worthy successor to Ficino. Thirty years younger than Ficino, they first met in 1484, supposedly on the day that Ficino published his translations of Plato, which greatly impressed the astrologer in him. Tall, good-looking and confident, Pico seems to have charmed everyone with whom he came in contact--in Florence at least. He was also precocious when it came to languages; he knew Latin and Greek of course, but also Hebrew, Arabic and Aramaic, and was widely read in the philosophical and religious texts native to them. He quickly became Ficino's student.

But either because of his youth or his temperament, he did not possess the same single-mindedness toward philosophy. He fell into an affair with the wife of one of Lorenzo's cousins and was almost killed as a result--it took a personal intervention on Lorenzo's part to prevent it. Also while in Florence he improbably became fast friends with the severely ascetic Savonarola, and would eventually choose him over his Platonist friends.

In 1486, when he was twenty-three, he produced the works for which he is most remembered: a set of 900 theses intended to show the common roots of all religions and philosophies, as well as *An Oration on the Dignity of Man,* which was intended to defend them. While it is a landmark text in humanism, extolling the wonders of man and his powers, it nonetheless places him in a hierarchy of being and admits of his ability to ascend to its top--to realize union with the Supreme Being.

For, raised to the most eminent height of theology, whence we shall be able to measure with the rod of indivisible eternity all things that are and that have been; and, grasping the primordial beauty of things, like the seers of Phoebus, we shall become the winged lovers of theology. And at last, smitten by the ineffable love as by a sting, and, like the Seraphim, filled with the godhead, we shall be, no longer ourselves, but the very One who made us.5

In 1487 he traveled to Rome, audaciously throwing down a challenge to all comers to debate him. But naturally the church, in the person of Pope Innocent VIII did not take to being lumped together with any pagan schools, and some of the theses were declared heretical. Pico was forced to retract them, which he did, but with his fingers crossed. An *Apology* he wrote defending himself was also found to contain heresies, and Pico fled to France where he was tracked down and imprisoned. Again it took the intervention of Lorenzo to get him released, and only on the understanding that Pico would live in Florence under Lorenzo's watchful eye.

He continued to write under this benign form of house arrest until Lorenzo's death in 1492, but grew more and more under the harsh influence of Savonarola, as did much of Florence. He died in 1494 at the age of 31 under mysterious circumstances; a suspicion has persisted that he was poisoned by surviving members of the Medici family because of his close ties to Savonarola. His extreme nature had swung back the other way, and he forgot what he had written in the *Oration* about the precepts of the Delphic oracle:

> As a matter of fact that aphorism: *meden agan,* this is: "Nothing in excess," duly prescribes a measure and rule for all the virtues through the concept of the "Mean" of which moral philosophy treats. In like manner, that other aphorism, *gnothi seauton,* that is, "Know thyself," invites and exhorts us to the study of the whole nature of which the nature of man is the connecting link and the "mixed potion"; for he who knows himself knows all things in himself, as Zoroaster first and after him Plato, in the Alcibiades, wrote. Finally, enlightened by this knowledge, through the aid of natural philosophy, being already close to God, employing the theological salutation *ei,* that is "Thou art," we shall blissfully address the true Apollo on intimate terms.

Ficino also maintained relationships with many intellectuals throughout Europe through the exchange of letters, presumably a side benefit of the wide-ranging Medici banking enterprise. And although most of these letters were intended for publication (Ficino had copies made as they were written) they still reveal a more personal and candid side than do his scholarly works. They are frequently written to one individual, known personally to Ficino, about one topic of immediate practical interest. The same sense of being personally addressed by Ficino still comes through in reading them today. (All the quotes below are taken from the collection of letters published under the title *Meditations on the Soul.*[6])

I've already spoken of the ascendance of humanism; the redefinition of the human being not as a miserable sinner, but as the noblest being in the creation. This idea was expressed perhaps most thoroughly by Pico, but Ficino also espoused it.

It was not for small things but for great that God[7] created men, who, knowing the great, are not satisfied with small things. Indeed, it was for the limitless alone that He created men, who are the only beings on earth to have rediscovered their infinite nature and who are not fully satisfied by anything limited, however great that thing may be. MOS 12

At the same time, he was all too aware of the tendency of humans to ignore their "infinite nature," and concentrate on the limited and illusory world of the sensible.

I can only judge it the most foolish act of all, that many people most diligently feed a beast, that is, their body, a wild, cruel, and dangerous animal;

but allow themselves, that is, the soul, insofar as they have one, to starve to death. MOS 19

How many people will you find who value a man as much as money; who cultivate themselves in the same way as they cultivate their fields and other affairs; who bring up their family with as much care as many rear their horses, dogs, and birds; who consider how grave is the waste of time? In spending money we are very mean, in spending time we are extravagant beyond measure. How many can you name who recognize the poverty of their soul? Everyone believes he abounds in wisdom, but is short of money. MOS 20

But he believed that philosophy had the ability to bring people back to their divine nature. The following is an excerpt from a letter written to Lorenzo de Medici. (Keep in mind that not only is Lorenzo now Ficino's patron, but one of the richest and most powerful men in Europe.)

What therefore is to be done, so that we may be of good strength and good vigilance? Life for us should straightway be turned right round in the opposite direction. Those things which we have learned from the many should be unlearned; in having to learn which, we have up to now ignored our own selves. Those things left undone should be learned; the which having been ignored we cannot know ourselves. What we neglect should be esteemed, what we esteem should be neglected. What we flee from, should be borne, what we pursue should be fled. For us the smile of fortune should bring tears; and the tears of fortune should bring a smile. For by these means, the filth of the multitude will not defile us, nor will carelessness of immortal things harm us, nor desire for knowledge of mortal things torment us. Weakness will not prostrate us, nor desire undo us. Neither will prosperous fortune ensnare us, nor adverse fortune slay us. But, insofar as we shall be cleansed, so shall we be serene; insofar as we shall be serene, so shall we shine. Then, for the first time, we shall go forth full of true beauty, when for the first time we are devoid of dreams. MOS 28

Like Plato and Plotinus, Ficino did not believe that philosophy was an abstract study, cut off from daily life. It requires right living, as well as a large measure of what is usually translated as "leisure." (*Otium,* of which the opposite is *negotium,* root of *negotiate.*) This is not leisure in the sense we use it today, but the time and ability to bring the mind to rest from its "busyness," (which, it may be a surprise to learn, is not a twenty-first century invention). It's this activity of the mind, tied to the senses, which keeps it limited and in the thrall of the changeable and transitory. It is only through the ability to still the mind that we will be able to come into the presence of The One, or unity.

We will not find the goal we seek in toil, but in rest, for we are endlessly busy to enjoy leisure, and wage war to live in peace. Besides, right conduct is never sought for its own sake but to put to use, like a medicine, for cleansing and calming the mind. Neither is Epicurean peace the ultimate goal. For the use of a still mind is the contemplation of truth, as the use of a clear sky is to admit light. MOS 59

Perhaps it would be worthwhile, if we wish to attain what we are seeking, to flee only to that which does not flee anywhere. But that alone cannot flee anywhere which cannot be moved anywhere, since it fills the universe. However, is there any need even to be moved to that which is not moved anywhere, which is present everywhere in every single thing? Then let us not be moved or distracted by many things, but let us remain in unity as much as we are able, since we find eternal unity and the one eternity, not through movement or multiplicity, but through being still and being one. MOS 67

Ficino's "good company" was not just in the world of his letters, however. As Clement Salaman states in his introduction to *Meditations on the Soul,* "It is clear that Ficino soon gathered around him a group of like-minded men, which he referred to as the Academy. How this group met and what happened at such meetings is far from clear." It is possible though that unwritten teachings, *agrapha dogmata*, were given of the kind to which Plato alludes in his Seventh Letter.

What is clear is that Ficino believed this search for the Good to be the reason for our being on earth; not, as it has been said, that we are human beings seeking a spiritual experience, but rather that we are spiritual beings having a human experience. The way for us to remember this he states quite clearly in a letter in which he assumes the voice of God.

It is not difficult to find the place where I am; for in me are all things, out of me come all things and by me are all things sustained forever and everywhere. And with infinite power I expand through infinite space. Indeed no place can be found where I am not; this very "where" surely exists through me and is called "everywhere." Whatever anyone does anywhere, he does through my guidance and my light. Whatever anyone seeks anywhere, he seeks through my guidance and my light. There is no desiring anywhere, except for the good; there is no finding anywhere, except of the truth. I am all good; I am all truth. Seek my face and you shall live. But do not move in order to touch me, for I am stillness itself. Do not be drawn in many directions in order to take hold of me; I am unity itself. Stop the movement, unify diversity, and you will surely reach me, who long ago reached you. MOS 29

[1] Marsilio Ficino, *Meditations on the Soul*, translated by members of the Language Department of the School of Economic Science, London, Clement Salaman, ed. Inner Traditions, 1996

[2] Marsilio Ficino, *De Sole*, trans. by Geoffry Cornelius et. al., *Sphinx 6: A Journal for Archetypal Psychology and the Arts*, 1994

[3] Sir Peter Hall, *Cities in Civilization*, Pantheon, 1998

[4] "Ficino's doctrine of immortality, and his arguments for it, made a profound impression on many thinkers of the sixteenth century, and it may well be due to his indirect influence that the immortality of the soul was formally pronounced a dogma of the Catholic Church at the Lateran council of 1512." Paul Oscar Kristeller, *Eight Philosophers of the Italian Renaissance*, Stanford, 1964

[5] Giovanni Pico della Mirandola, *Oration on the Dignity of Man*

[6] Salaman, trans., op. cit.

[7] As befits someone who wrote, "But truth and wisdom itself, are God alone, so it follows that lawful Philosophy is no different from true religion, and lawful religion exactly the same as true Philosophy," (MOS 48) Ficino uses the words the One, the Good, Unity, and God interchangeably. May we not let our limited and stereotyped concepts of this last be an impediment to our understanding of what he is really saying.

Chapter X: Platonic Beauty in the Renaissance

Michelangelo

It is easy to see the appeal of Idealism to artists: it provides an embrace of beauty not typically found in religions, and elevates it to a status as inherent in the Good. Seeking beauty, which is what an artist does, is therefore seeking the divine, although many artists are content to stop far short of it. And like anything else, the creation of art can become a tool of the ego, used to bring attention to the artist, rather than the existence of beauty itself.

But this was never the case with Michelangelo, about whom Emerson said: "He was not a citizen of any country ; he belonged to the human race ; he was a brother and a friend to all who acknowledge the beauty that beams in universal nature, and who seek by labor and self-denial to approach its source in perfect goodness." Michelangelo would no doubt be totally indifferent to Emerson's essay--or this one-- since his concern was never with his own reputation, but only with how he could better express the beauty of spirit he saw in nature, and especially in the human form. All his life he was a student of how the soul was expressed through the body (his motto in late life was "Ancora imparo," "I still learn") which earned him the right to be a spiritual teacher first, an artist second.

An advantage in featuring prose writers as proponents of the Ideal is that they can tell you, explicitly, that they are Idealists. With poets, as we'll see with Shakespeare, we may have to infer it, and with painters or sculptors the connection can become further hidden. In the person of Michelangelo, we have the case of a visual artist who also wrote poetry, so the link becomes more evident. As John Symonds says in the introduction to his translation of Michelangelo's sonnets,

> Nothing is more clear than that Michael Angelo worshiped beauty in the Platonic spirit, passing beyond its personal and specific manifestations to the universal and impersonal. This thought is repeated over and over again in his poetry; and if we bear in mind that he habitually regarded the loveliness of man or woman as a sign and symbol of eternal and immutable beauty, we shall feel it of less importance who it was that prompted him to this or that poetic utterance.[1]

(I think this is also all that needs to be said on the distraction of his sexual orientation.)

We know that Michelangelo was exposed to Plato and the Ideal tradition by the best that Florence had to offer. As Linda Murray points out,

> The young Michelangelo seems to have impressed Lorenzo (de Medici) since, as both Condivi and Vasari record, he took him into his household and brought him up with his own two sons, so that Michelangelo had the advantage of at least two years of surroundings which included the humanist Poliziano, tutor to Lorenzo's children. The foundations of his Neoplatonism and classical interests were laid here, under the influence of Poliziano and other celebrated humanists who visited the Medicean court: Marsilio Ficino, translator of Plato and source of the Platonic inspiration in Michelangelo's later

work; Cristophoro Landino, commentator on Virgil and Dante, and another link in the Neoplatonic chain of thought; Pico della Mirandola, humanist, profound scholar of Plato and Aristotle, and the man who attempted to reconcile the Bible with Platonic philosophy.[2]

The exact influence of this education on Michelangelo will probably never be known, but he certainly possessed a single-mindedness of purpose that few other artists then or since have exhibited. He was driven to work long hours without food or sleep, and was solitary and often anti-social. He was paranoid, arrogant and combative. He maintained no studio and few assistants. All he was went into the work.

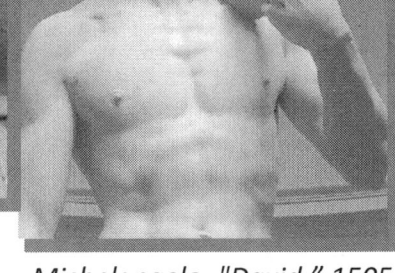

Michelangelo, "Pieta" (detail), 1498-99   *Michelangelo, "David," 1505*

Everything he put his eye and hand to revealed his love of beauty; sculptures, paintings, architecture. They seemed to flow from him like breath. His early works such as the Pieta and David are astonishing in their mastery and simplicity. There is no showing off, no flourishes that take the attention away from the emotional statement. Here is the calm sorrow of a mother contemplating the mystery of a son who is dead and yet lives. Here is the fearless inner stillness of one who knows he is joined to The One.

His verse is not so fluid; he is reaching for Beauty, but not quite grasping it. To quote Symonds again, "Michael Angelo has the obscurity of a writer whose thoughts exceed his power of expression, and who complicates the verbal form by his endeavour to project what cannot easily be said in verse."[3]

Two examples will serve.

XIV. First Reading.

TO VITTORIA COLONNA.

THE MODEL AND THE STATUE.

Da che concetto.

When divine Art conceives a form and face,

She bids the craftsman for his first essay

To shape a simple model in mere clay:

This is the earliest birth of Art's embrace.

From the live marble in the second place

His mallet brings into the light of day

A thing so beautiful that who can say

When time shall conquer that immortal grace?

Thus my own model I was born to be—

The model of that nobler self, whereto

Schooled by your pity, lady, I shall grow.

Each overplus and each deficiency

You will make good. What penance then is due

For my fierce heat, chastened and taught by you?

Although the immediate dedication is to Vittoria Colonna, we can hear the appeal to the source of his "nobler self," that which radiates "immortal grace." It brings to mind Plotinus' analogy of our being our own sculptors, "If you do not as yet see beauty within you, do as does the sculptor of a statue that is to be beautified: he cuts away here, he smooths it there, he makes this line lighter, this one purer, until he disengages beautiful lineaments in the marble."[4]

XXIX.   Love's Dilemma

I' mi credetti.

I deemed upon that day when first I knew

So many peerless beauties blent in one,

That, like an eagle gazing on the sun,

Mine eyes might fix on the least part of you.

That dream hath vanished, and my hope is flown;

For he who fain a seraph would pursue

Wingless, hath cast words to the winds, and dew

On stones, and gauged God's reason with his own.

If then my heart cannot endure the blaze

Of beauties infinite that blind these eyes,

Nor yet can bear to be from you divided,

What fate is mine? Who guides or guards my ways,

Seeing my soul, so lost and ill-betided,

Burns in your presence, in your absence dies?

Like so many of Shakespeare's sonnets, this one, addressed to the "peerless beauties blent in one," is about the times when we feel alienated from it. We have lost the ability even to see "the least part of you," because we have "gauged God's reason with (our) own," that is, we try to "understand" noesis with dianoia, in the terminology of the Divided Line. Although Michelangelo may have sometimes lost this connection, he never mistook the one for the other.

So we have a case of a man who was not content with the riches and fame that his talent commanded. He was not impressed with popes and kings and other artists. He felt kinship only with those who shared his love of beauty, such as Vittoria Colonna. Whether he continued to read Plato or Plotinus I can't say, but it's obvious to me that he lived his life in the realm of the Good, and filed a lifetime of reports that continue to speak to us after 500 years, and which always will. We have the case of a man who knew, as did Diotima, that "in that communion only, beholding beauty with the eye of the mind, he will be enabled to bring forth, not images of beauty, but realities..., and bringing forth and nourishing true virtue to become the friend of God and be immortal, if mortal man may."

Botticelli

Allesandro (Sandro) Botticelli (nee Filipepi) (1445-1510) was born in Florence twelve years after Marsilio Ficino, and while there doesn't seem to be any proof (or disproof) that he "belonged" to Ficino's Academy, it is obvious that he was influenced by the Neoplatonism that Academy promulgated. He knew and painted many members of the Medici family, as well as the student of Ficino, Pico della Mirandola, and other humanists who were part of it.

Perhaps more than any other artist of the time, Botticelli chose as his subjects themes from ancient Greek and Roman mythologies. He also painted many pictures of strictly Christian iconography, and apparently--at least in the early part of his career--did not see any conflict between them. In his later life he became a disciple of the austere monk Savonarola, essentially stopped painting, and and is said to have burned some of his own earlier works in the "bonfires of the vanities."

While debate still goes on about the meanings of these Greek-inspired works to us today, it is evident that they speak a language with which the Florentines of the 15th century were more familiar. An example is the famous "Birth of Venus," which now hangs in the

Ufizzi Gallery. It seems to be derived from the Greek myth of the birth of Aphrodite (Ἀφροδίτη), in which she was born when the severed genitals of the sky-god Uranus (or Ouranos, Οὐρανός) were thrown into the sea by his son Cronos. Without getting too graphic, Aphrodite was born from that fertilization, if you will. Whereas the Greek Aphrodite was associated just with sexual passion, the Roman Venus was more complex, and also had associations with beauty and love.

"The Birth of Venus," by Sandro Botticelli, 1484

In the painting, Venus is naked, but is making something of an attempt to cover her nakedness. She is born out of the sea, carried on a seashell, and is being propelled toward land by a winged wind-blowing god and nymph, perhaps.5 On the right, a clothed woman stands ready to cover Venus as she moves to the land. This can be seen as an Ideal of Beauty at the moment of crossing the border, as in the Divided Line, from the Intelligible to the Sensible, from the divine to the mundane, from the universal to the particular. Around the wind-spirits, flowers swirl freely, while on the right, they have become static images, woven into the cloth. So I believe this painting is representative of that transitional moment with which we humans are always faced: are we creatures of the intellect or of the senses? Can we be spiritually naked, like Adam and Eve also, or must we always be covered with the cloth, however beautiful, of our own limited identities?

Raphael

Raphael Sanzio (1483-1520), one of Michelangelo's rivals, was born in the wrong place (Urbino) and came to Florence too late (probably 1504) to participate in the Platonic Academy. By then, it and the Medici and Michelangelo were gone. But he did absorb the influence of the art that was everywhere, and especially came under the influence of Leonardo, who had returned to Florence around this time. This influence can be seen in his use of landscapes in portraits, which of course is a hallmark of Leonardo's--Michelangelo had no use for them, putting all the attention on the person, which even in his paintings look like sculptures. Raphael, wisely did not attempt sculpture, leaving that turf to Michelangelo alone.

But Raphael's talent was obvious, and soon he headed to Rome where he was also employed by Pope Julian II in decorating his quarters at the Vatican. Michelangelo was at work nearby on the Sistine Chapel under great secrecy, but it is said that sometimes at night Raphael would be let in so he could view the dynamic, muscular figures that populated Michelangelo's vision. Raphael, more generous in his evaluation of other artists, included Michelangelo in his famous work, the "School of Athens," which also shows his intimate knowledge of the Ideal tradition. Michelangelo is cast as Heraclitus in the front, while Plato has the face of Leonardo. (If the figure of Socrates was based on another artist, no one seems to know now who it was.)

"The School of Athens," by Raphael Sanzio, 1511

The tradition is here recognized and validated in a way it never had been before. Pre-Socratic philosophers are included, as well as Plotinus (the brown-robed figure on the right) and some non-Western writers such as Averroes who had also contributed to the tradition. Raphael's knowledge of the tradition is astonishingly complete, and could only have been acquired based on the translations of Plato, Plotinus and others by Ficino. It is also remarkable for having only "pagan" figures of the tradition, where one might reasonably expect to see Christian Platonists such as St. Augustine included, especially in the private chambers of the pope. Of this painting, Sir Kenneth Clark says, in *Civilisation: A Personal View*

> The Stanza della Segnature was to be the Pope's private library. Raphael knew the library at Urbino where paintings of poets, philosophers and theologians were placed above the shelves containing their books, and he determined to carry out the same idea much further. He would not only portray the figures whose books were in the shelves below, but would relate them to each other and the whole discipline of which they formed a part. He must have had advice from the learned and cultivated men who made up about a third of the papal curia. But this sublime work wasn't assembled by a committee. Everything in the group is thought out. For example, of the two central figures in the School of Athens, Plato the idealist is on the left, and he points upwards to divine inspiration. Beyond him to the left are the philosophers who appealed to intuition and the emotions. They are nearer the figure of Apollo-- and they lead on to the wall of the Parnassus. To the right is Aristotle, the man of good sense, holding out a moderating hand; and beyond him are the representatives of rational activities-- logic, grammar and geometry. [6]

As Clark mentions, not content to stop there, on the wall to the left Raphael painted another mural based on a Greek theme, that of the great names of poetry gathering on Mount Parnassus. At the center is Apollo (Ἀπόλλων, "not many"), along with Calliope (or Kalliope, Καλλιόπη, "beautiful-voiced"), inspirers of music and poetry, surrounded by other muses and great poets from Greece and Italy. It must have been a relief to sit in the presence of these serene and happy paintings, given the often grim and joyless subject matter found in Bible stories.

[1]John Addington Symonds, trans., *The Sonnets of Michael Angelo Buonarroti*, available at:

http://www.gutenberg.org/ebooks/10314

[2]Linda Murray, *Michelangelo (World of Art)*, Thames and Hudson, 1980

[3]Symonds, op. cit.

[4]The complete analogy, as seen in Chapter 6, "How can one see the beauty of a good soul?" Withdraw into yourself and look. If you do not as yet see beauty within you, do as does the sculptor of a statue that is to be beautified: he cuts away here, he smooths it there, he makes this line lighter, this one purer, until he disengages beautiful lineaments in the marble. Do you this, too. Cut away all that is excessive, straighten all that is crooked, bring light to all that is overcast, labor to make all one radiance of beauty. Never cease "working at the statue" until there shines out upon you from it the divine sheen of virtue, until you see perfect "goodness firmly established in the stainless shrine."

[5]The cat-tails in the lower left of the picture are obviously phallic symbols. Kidding!

[6]Kenneth Clark, *Civilisation: A Personal View*, Harper and Row, 1969, p. 181. (I'm not entirely sure I buy this, given that Plotinus is also in this "Aristotelian" group. Also, of course he had access to learned men other than those in the papal curia.)

Chapter XI: Shakespeare, the Cambridge Platonists and Thomas Taylor

The sixteenth century was truly revolutionary, bringing Renaissance ideas to all of Europe.

A major force was the tremendous spread of printing and "democratization" of books, perhaps the most influential being Martin Luther's translation of the Bible from Latin into vernacular German. Implicit in this publication was the principle that the text was no longer just for the clergy--that anyone who could read, or be read to, had access to "the Word of God." This of course is one of the empowering principles of Renaissance humanism.

As Protestantism spread, mostly across Northern Europe, there was a commensurate rise in the growth of universities. Universities that had been established for the training of priests changed their religion and their faculties, but still retained the basic orientation toward producing clergymen. (That it was all clergy*men* of course goes without saying.) Over time, though, they tended to become more secular, offering programs in medicine and law that helped in the development of those professions.

Philosophy was taught as a core component of the liberal arts, but gradually it came to be done so as another academic subject, not as a way of life. It came to appeal to what Plato, in the Divided Line, called *dianoia;* the realm of the mind that can, but only, understand. Its overarching assumption is that all things can be reduced to thought-objects which can then be made subject to disputation and proofs. Consequently during this time there arose a cottage industry among academics of publications countering arguments by other academics who then reply to them. The language used when speaking of the Good became the language of the pedant, without the poetry and direct experience of Plotinus or Ficino. Plato and other ancient philosophers became raw material for academic oneupmanship, rather than teachers of how to live a just life and realize unity with The One.

But this knowledge continued on, outside the academic establishment. I must admit I write this chapter with some trepidation, since the connections to the Ideal in Shakespeare are not as clear as they are among other writers. At times they seem to be self-evident; at others, you wonder what he could possibly be thinking. To me it gives some credence to the idea that there were several Shakespeares, one with a clear view of "Beauty Absolute," and any number of hacks who are content to construct the artful little pieces of fluff that he otherwise seems to despise. But face it: all of Shakespearean scholarship is wild speculation, and this speculation is no wilder than most.[1]

That said, the presence of "Ideal" themes in Shakespeare, both in the plays and the sonnets, becomes evident once it is revealed.[2] In many of the "king" plays especially, we see the theme of the rightful ruler (Lear, King Hamlet, Duncan, everybody in *Richard III*) who is overthrown, often murdered, and whose kingship is usurped by a pretender. The result of course is always disastrous, not only for the pretenders but everyone else as well until a new legitimate ruler reappears. Read in a psychological light (and with the original meaning of "psyche" as "soul"), we can see that these are allegories of the soul in the way Plato's Republic is: the state is the soul writ large. When we permit our true identity as The Good to be usurped by the ego, we invite disaster. It's fine for the ego, but we pay the price in a feeling of mortality and meaninglessness:

> To-morrow, and to-morrow, and to-morrow,
> Creeps in this petty pace from day to day,
> To the last syllable of recorded time;
> And all our yesterdays have lighted fools
> The way to dusty death. Out, out, brief candle!
> Life's but a walking shadow, a poor player,
> That struts and frets his hour upon the stage,
> And then is heard no more. It is a tale
> Told by an idiot, full of sound and fury,
> Signifying nothing. (Macbeth, Act V, sc. 5)

As pure an expression of the ego's creed as has ever been put to paper. But in other plays Shakespeare can give expression to the Ideal itself, here through the person of Juliet Capulet, in the famous balcony scene:

> And yet I wish but for the thing I have:
> My bounty is as boundless as the sea,
> My love as deep; the more I give to thee,
> The more I have, for both are infinite. (Romeo and Juliet, Act 2, sc. 2)

But here I'd like to concentrate on the sonnets as more manageable in scope. Traditional scholarship has seen them as addressed to the "fair youth" or the "dark lady," and there are many of them that do seem addressed to a certain person on a certain theme. The first dozen or so, the "procreation" sonnets in particular, go on to the point of tediousness trying to encourage the young man to father a child.[3] But interspersed there are some that speak to something much larger and more enduring than an individual, to a vision of love and beauty that is not just poetic hyperbole.

I see it first in Sonnet 29, and its companion piece Sonnet 30. In both we hear the voice of a man who is being tortured by ego, in the form of thoughts of dissatisfaction and envy, or in the case of #30, of memory and regret. But in both cases, when "I think on thee," he is returned to the present and to happiness.

> #29
> When, in disgrace with fortune and men's eyes,
> I all alone beweep my outcast state
> And trouble deaf heaven with my bootless cries
> And look upon myself and curse my fate,
> Wishing me like to one more rich in hope,
> Featured like him, like him with friends
>   possess'd,
> Desiring this man's art and that man's scope,
> With what I most enjoy contented least;
> Yet in these thoughts myself almost despising,
> Haply I think on thee, and then my state,
> Like to the lark at break of day arising
> From sullen earth, sings hymns at heaven's gate;
> For thy sweet love remember'd such wealth
>   brings
> That then I scorn to change my state with kings.

#30

When to the sessions of sweet silent thought
I summon up remembrance of things past,
I sigh the lack of many a thing I sought,
And with old woes new wail my dear time's
    waste:
Then can I drown an eye, unused to flow,
For precious friends hid in death's dateless night,
And weep afresh love's long since cancell'd woe,
And moan the expense of many a vanish'd sight:
Then can I grieve at grievances foregone,
And heavily from woe to woe tell o'er
The sad account of fore-bemoanèd moan,
Which I new pay as if not paid before.
But if the while I think on thee, dear friend,
All losses are restored and sorrows end.

Now of course a thought of the fair youth could bring about this change, but there is the sense of something beyond the personal, certainly not romantic, about the "dear friend" that can bring about so complete a change of heart.

The key question becomes: Who is "thee?" Or "you," as in Sonnet 76 where he says,

    "O! know sweet love I always write of you,
    And you and love are still my argument"

While some of the sonnets have the lover's fickleness as their theme, often it is the reverse--its constancy and endurance as the source of all in the visible realm, as the sun is the Child of the Good. It evokes an unchangeableness that transcends the comparative metaphoric structure of tenor and vehicle. These are different levels of reality, as in the segments of the

Divided Line. In Sonnet 53, Shakespeare invokes Plato's imagery of shadows, and the physical world as the "counterfeit" of the Ideal.

> What is your substance, whereof are you made,
> That millions of strange shadows on you tend?
> Since every one hath, every one, one shade,
> And you but one, can every shadow lend.
> Describe Adonis, and the counterfeit
> Is poorly imitated after you;
> On Helen's cheek all art of beauty set,
> And you in Grecian tires are painted new:
> Speak of the spring, and foison of the year,
> The one doth shadow of your beauty show,
> The other as your bounty doth appear;
> And you in every blessèd shape we know.
> In all external grace you have some part,
> But you like none, none you, for constant heart.

I think it is quite evident that we are not talking about a person here. And although the "you" is constant, our experience of it is not. In the sequence from 97 through 99, Shakespeare speaks of the experience of beautiful things seen without the Beauty Absolute.

Here is # 98:
From you have I been absent in the spring,
When proud-pied April dress'd in all his trim
Hath put a spirit of youth in every thing
That heavy Saturn laugh'd and leap'd with him.
Yet nor the lays of birds nor the sweet smell
Of different flowers in odor and in hue
Could make me any summer's story tell.
Or from their proud lap pluck them while they grew;

Nor did I wonder at the lily's white,
Nor praise the deep vermilion in the rose;
These were but sweet, but figures of delight;
Drawn after you, you pattern of all those.
Yet seem'd it winter still, and, you away,
As with your shadow I with these did play.

But when the shadows are seen as such, and the light itself returns, the poet shares in its constancy and the experience of beauty, love and truth coming together in Unity.

Sonnet 105:
Let not my love be called idolatry,
Nor my beloved as an idol show,
Since all alike my songs and praises be
To one, of one, still such, and ever so.
Kind is my love to-day, to-morrow kind,
Still constant in a wondrous excellence;
Therefore my verse to constancy confined,
One thing expressing, leaves out difference.
Fair, kind, and true, is all my argument,
Fair, kind, and true, varying to other words;
And in this change is my invention spent,
Three themes in one, which wondrous scope
    affords.
Fair, kind, and true, have often lived alone,
Which three till now, never kept seat in one.

The Cambridge Platonists

In the seventeenth century though the connection to the Ideal tradition becomes clear. At Cambridge University there arose a group of men (and one woman, Anne Conway) who will forever be lumped together as the Cambridge Platonists. Like Ficino, most also had a background in Christian theology, and saw no conflict between the two. Their original writings are hard to come by these days, even given the Internet, but Sarah Hutton, in her excellent overview in the Stanford Encyclopedia of Philosophy says:

> The framework within which they read and understood ancient and modern philosophy was that of the 'perennial philosophy' (*philosophia perennis*) proposed originally by Italian Renaissance philosophers such as Marsilio Ficino, and Agostino Steucho[4], but also employed by Gottfried Wilhelm Leibniz. Not only did they share the Renaissance Humanist regard for the achievements of ancient philosophy, but like the Humanists of the Renaissance, their interest was dictated by their sense of the relevance of classical philosophy to contemporary life. They also emphatically repudiated the scholasticism that prevailed in academic philosophy and took a lively interest in the developments that brought about the scientific revolution.[5]

Perhaps because they wrote in English, not Latin, or because "Platonism" was falling out of favor with the academics always in search of something new, their influence was not very wide or lasting. (Why it does not seem to have occurred to any of them to translate Plato into English is something we will never know.) But they did help to set the stage for one who, although not an academic, and largely unappreciated in his own country, nonetheless left a legacy which reached to America and today: Thomas Taylor.

Taylor was born in 1758, a full century after most of the Cambridge Platonists had died. His father was a minister, and intended Thomas to be the same, but Thomas seems to have had a strong sense of another mission from an early age and rebelled against this idea. In the grueling course of his education, apprenticeships, and self-study, he did learn Greek and Latin, as well as pursue a fascination for mathematics. He further guaranteed his poverty by marrying his childhood sweetheart, Mary Morton, at the age of 19, incurring the wrath of her parents and cutting themselves off from any dowry. (It is said that they spoke to each other only in ancient Greek.) At some point, he decided to become the English Ficino and translate all the ancient Greek works he could find, although he had no Medici to support the enterprise. Eventually, however, he did become acquainted with patrons who supported the work, as well as obtaining a post at the Society for the Encouragement of Art, precursor to the Royal Society of Arts. He also became a member of an "academy" that included his patron William Meredith, the artist John Flaxman, and probably the poet and artist William Blake.

As with Ficino, it is evident in reading his original works that his appreciation went beyond that of a translator. Unfortunately, his gift for language is that of a mathematician. Sarah Hutton says of Ralph Cudworth, his "...baroque style...occluded the originality of his contribution to English philosophy and helped to ensure his undeserved neglect...."[6] The same can be said for Taylor. In his own lifetime Coleridge wrote that Taylor had translated Proclus' "difficult Greek into incomprehensible English,"[7] and that, combined with his lack of academic *bona fides,* limited his influence in England.

It was in America, unencumbered by such class distinctions, that Taylor had his real influence. Ralph Waldo Emerson, although he knew Greek from Harvard, was nonetheless a fan of Taylor's translations. On his second trip to England in 1848, he met with William Wordsworth and recorded later in his book *English Traits,* "We talked of English national characteristics. I told him it was not creditable that no one in all the country knew anything of Thomas Taylor, the Platonist, while in every American library his translations are to be found."[8] (Oddly, it does not appear that Emerson sought Taylor out on his first trip to England in 1831, even though he was still alive.) Emerson writes of Taylor with great admiration in other essays as well. Bronson Alcott, Emerson's friend and inspiration, also claimed his introduction to Plato via Taylor as a red-letter day in his life.

So for better or worse, here is what Taylor has to say in his *Introduction to the Philosophy and Writings of Platonists:*

> "Philosophy," says Hierocles, "is the purification and perfection of human life. It is the purification, indeed, from material irrationality, and the mortal body; but the perfection, in consequence of being the resumption of our proper felicity, and a reascent to the divine likeness. To effect these two is the province of Virtue and Truth; the former exterminating the

immoderation of the passions; and the latter introducing the divine form to those who are naturally adapted to its reception."

Of philosophy thus defined, which may be compared to a luminous pyramid, terminating in Deity, and having for its basis the rational soul of man and its spontaneous unperverted conceptions,--of this philosophy, August, magnificent, and divine, Plato may be justly called the primary leader and hierophant, through whom, like the mystic light in the inmost recesses of some sacred temple, it first shone forth with occult and venerable splendour. It may indeed be truly said of the whole of this philosophy, that it is the greatest good in which man can participate: for if it purifies us from the defilements of the passions and assimilates us to Divinity, it confers on us the proper felicity of our nature. Hence it is easy to collect its pre-eminence to all other philosophies; to show that where they oppose it, they are erroneous; that so far as they contain any thing scientific they are allied to it; and that at best they are but rivulets derived from this vast ocean of truth.[9]

In the next chapter we will follow the Ideal as it continues its westward march, and installs itself in the person of Ralph Waldo Emerson.

[1]For some quite wild speculation, there is John Kerrigan's introduction to The Sonnets and A Lover's Complaint (Penguin Classics). On p. 52 he claims, "Shakespeare, of course, was not a neoplatonist. He was painfully aware of the way the ideals like Ficino's are corrupted in practice, and of how imponderable true beauty is in the soul." I would suggest that for the first, one can be aware of the corruption (as was Ficino) and still be a Neoplatonist, and for the second, that in most of the sonnets he is in fact precisely pondering the beauty of the soul.

[2]For a comprehensive survey of the Ideal as it is portrayed in the plays, see John Vyvyan, *The Shakespearean Ethic,* Shepheard-Walwyn, 2011. A companion work that makes explicit his debt to Plato is *Shakespeare and Platonic Beauty,* which is available at forgottenbooks.org

[3]Although even here, Shakespeare is showing a Platonist strain, as evidenced by the following from Diotima's speech in The Symposium: "There is a certain age at which human nature is desirous of procreation — procreation which must be in beauty and not in deformity; and this procreation is the union of man and woman, and is a divine thing; for conception and generation are an immortal principle in the mortal creature, and in the inharmonious they can never be. "

[4]sic. Most sources spell his name Steuco. He is an interesting character in his own right, born just two years before Ficino died, and the first to use the phrase in his work *De perenni philosophia libri X,* published in 1540.

[5]Sarah Hutton, The Cambridge Platonists, *The Stanford Encyclopedia of Philosophy.*

[6]Ibid.

[7]Quoted in Kathleen Raine and George Mills Harper, eds., Thomas Taylor the Platonist: Selected Writings, *Princeton University Press, 1969*

[8]Ralph Waldo Emerson, English Traits, *Ralph Waldo Emerson Institute,* rwe.org

[9]Thomas Taylor, in Kathleen Raine and George Mills Harper, eds., op. Cit.

Chapter XII: The Transcendentalists and Ralph Waldo Emerson

Ralph Waldo Emerson, 1803-1882

I think it's safe to say that when most people consider Ralph Waldo Emerson, they think of a rather avuncular producer of pithy quotes in an archaic style of writing. Although his words still pop up with fair frequency, especially now given the presence of online quotation catalogs, I also think it's safe to say that most people know little of Emerson's life, or his deep connection with and expression of the Ideal.[1] He is usually labeled a Transcendentalist[2], along with Thoreau and others of his circle, but he never warmed to that slightly condescending term. As he said in his lecture entitled *The Transcendentalist*, "The first thing we have to say respecting what are called 'new views' here in New England, at the present time, is, that they are not new, but the very oldest of thoughts cast into the mould of these new times.... What is popularly called Transcendentalism among us, is Idealism; Idealism as it appears in 1842."[3] He was very aware of the tradition we have been considering, and considered himself a humble bearer of it.

Emerson was born in Boston in 1803, to a respectable Congregationalist minister, William Emerson and his wife Ruth Haskins Emerson. He was the third of what would be six sons, and expectations for him were never very high. His father died when he was eight, and the genteelness of their poverty was thus taken away; the family was now just poor. But education and the life of the mind were still valued highly, and Waldo and his brothers would take turns attending the Boston Latin School, and being tutored by a remarkable collection of mostly women--family friends and relatives. The chief among these influences was his father's sister, Mary Moody Emerson, who Robert Richardson says "was an American Jakob Boehme. Her everyday life was spent wrestling with angels."[4] She would write, visit, and be a presence in Waldo's life until her death in 1863.

Waldo was accepted into Harvard at the age of fourteen and was able to attend by dint of a scholarship, working, and the support of his brother William. In his junior year he began to keep a journal, which he would continue to do almost to the end of his life. It soon became a repository for his deepest thoughts and his growing sense of the presence in his life of what he would later call "The Over-Soul." In it he is writing to himself for himself about himself. On December 21 1823 he writes, "I say to the Universe, Mighty one! thou art not my mother; return to chaos if thou wilt, I shall still exist. I live. If I owe my being, it is to a destiny greater than thine. Star by star, world by world, system by system shall be crushed--but I shall live."5

Waldo graduated in the middle of his class, still unsure of his vocation. His two older brothers had become teachers; he followed suit, and their pooled resources greatly helped the family's financial outlook. But he was still not satisfied. Just before turning twenty-one, he notes in his journal "I burn after the 'aliquid imensum infinitumque' ("something great and immeasurable") which Cicero desired." (April 18, 1824) While continuing to teach, Waldo returned to Harvard Divinity School and emerged "approbated to preach," in 1826. He had already established a reputation as a speaker by filling in various pulpits in New England, but he still suffered from what might be called an existential crisis: "My years are passing away. Infirmities are already stealing on me that may be the deadly enemies that are to dissolve me to dirt and little is yet done to establish my consideration among my contemporaries & less to get a memory when I am gone." (March 27, 1826)

He was also suffering from physical ill health, and the following winter he made a trip to Florida to help recover. There he reconnected with the unnameable: "There is a pleasure in the thought that the particular tone of my mind at this moment may be new in the Universe; that the emotions of this hour may be peculiar & unexampled in the whole eternity of moral being. I lead a new life. I occupy new ground in the world of spirits, untenanted before. I commence a career of thought & action which is expanding before me into a distant & dazzling infinity. Strange thoughts start up like angels in my way & beckon me onward. I doubt not I tread on the highway that leads to the divinity." (April 17, 1827)

Returning to New England he continued preaching and drawing admirers--including, while in Concord New Hampshire, the beautiful young Ellen Louisa Tucker. In December of 1828 they became engaged, and the following January Waldo was called to be minister of the Second Church of Boston, a prestigious post that also brought him a higher salary than he had ever known. He became the family's main breadwinner, then chaplain of the Massachusetts legislature, then member of the Boston school committee. As Richardson says, "Emerson the private person became more or less overnight a complete institutional person."[6]

But it wasn't to last. In February 1831, Ellen, always frail, then tubercular, died after a long illness. Her last words were, "I have not forgot the peace and joy." Emerson came undone. By the end of the year he resigned his ministry, sold his belongings, packed up his grief and boarded a ship bound for Europe.

His journeys started in the island of Malta, through Italy to France and then to England. While he was escaping from the pain of Boston, he was also entering into a new world of art and religious expression. He saw everything, he wrote in his journal, he met other writers. In Paris, while decrying it as "a loud modern New York of a place," he discovered at an exhibition at the *Jardin des Plantes* a fascination with the huge variety of the plant and animals worlds, and his relation to it. "I feel the centipede in me--cayman, carp, eagle, & fox. I am moved by strange sympathies, I say continually, 'I will be a naturalist.'" (July 13, 1833) He moved on to England, home of his own ancestors, met Wordsworth, Coleridge, and Thomas Carlyle, but oddly, as mentioned before, not Thomas Taylor. It is safe to say that at the end of his journey, he was renewed in body, mind and spirit. He returned to Boston in October of 1833, full of ideas for a new life.

He began writing furiously, but also returned to supply preaching. It was at one of these engagements that he met Lydia Jackson of Plymouth, whom he married in 1835, and they moved into the famous boxy white house on the Cambridge Turnpike in Concord. In 1836 his son Waldo was born and he also published his first book, *Nature,*[7] his ambitious attempt, it might be said, at a Grand Unified Theory.

> Undoubtedly we have no questions to ask which are unanswerable. We must trust the perfection of the creation so far, as to believe that whatever curiosity the order of things has awakened in our minds, the order of things can satisfy. Every man's condition is a solution in hieroglyphic to those inquiries he would put. He acts it as life, before he apprehends it as truth. In like manner, nature is already, in its forms and tendencies, describing its own design. Let us interrogate the

great apparition, that shines so peacefully around us. Let us inquire, to what end is nature?

Although "Nature" did not sell well initially, it was very influential among the *cognoscenti* of Boston, and soon Emerson found himself to be a favorite on the growing Lyceum lecture circuit. For about the next forty years he would spend a large part of his time on the road, lecturing, the other part writing and being with friends. He started a magazine, *The Dial*, with his friend Margaret Fuller, and became father to two daughters, Ellen and Edith. In 1841, his first book of *Essays* was published, which included some of his most famous works, *Self Reliance* and *The Over-Soul*, and his fame increased even more. It was a heady time, even more than his days at the Second Church, since now his life was on his own terms.

But now, as then, a death intervened. On January 27, 1842, his son Waldo died of scarlet fever at the age of 5. Three days later he wrote in his journal, "Sorrow makes us all children again, destroys all differences of intellect. The wisest know nothing." But while it would be wrong to minimize his grief--or, like some, to say that he lost his optimism--I believe he did retain his knowledge of the Good; the Good as that which endures, which is eternal, of which the body is a relic.

We will look at Emerson's reactions to these deaths more fully in the chapter on The Ideal and the Art of Dying.

Of all the philosophers we have considered, Emerson was the most "in the world." We have not had time to look at many large aspects of his life--his abolitionist activities, his own Idealist circle, his poetry and friendships--but they can serve to instruct us that it is not necessary to withdraw from the world in order to know the Ideal. It was the foundation of his life, the medium through which he moved and in which he rested. And while he offers many profound descriptions of the Ideal--indeed he is often working at the edge of what is expressible--perhaps his most profound evidence is in his gift for the simple, unadorned, but penetrating Observation. In his journal, March 29 1869, he records a meeting with his dear friend Bronson Alcott.

> Alcott came & talked Plato & Socrates, extolling them with gravity. I bore it long, & then said, that was a song for others, not for him. He should find what was the equivalent for these masters in our times: for surely the world was always equal to itself, & it was for him to detect what was the counter-weight & compensation to us. Was it natural science? Was it the immense dilution of the same amount of thought into nations?
>
> I told him to shut his eyes, & let his thoughts run into reverie or whithersoever--& then take an observation. He would find that the current went outward from man, not to man. Consciousness was up stream.

Emerson's writing

The first thing we have to say respecting Emerson as a subject for writing about the Ideal is that we are aware of the irony. He spent his whole life trying to convince humanity that each of us is the Ideal, individually wrapped, and yet we persist in thinking it's about him. But he himself used the examples of Plato, Shakespeare, Goethe and other "representative men" to make his points, so I feel safe in doing the same.[8] Just remember to look at the moon, not his pointing finger.

I've already quoted from his essay *The Transcendentalist* in which he makes explicit his connection to the Idealist tradition, and certainly I encourage you to read the entire essay. But another excerpt here would serve as valuable distinction between it and materialism, to show Emerson's appreciation of consciousness as the prior reality.

> The idealist, in speaking of events, sees them as spirits. He does not deny the sensuous fact: by no means; but he will not see that alone. He does not deny the presence of this table, this chair, and the walls of this room, but he looks at these things as the reverse side of the tapestry, as the "other end," each being a sequel or completion of a spiritual fact which nearly concerns him. This manner of looking at things, transfers every object in nature from an independent and anomalous position without there, into the consciousness. Even the materialist Condillac, perhaps the most logical expounder of materialism, was constrained to say, "Though we should soar into the heavens, though we should sink into the abyss, we never go out of ourselves; it is always our own thought that we perceive." What more could an idealist say?

This was written in 1842, but as we've seen his experience of the Ideal goes back much further, and permeates his first published work *Nature,* which, as

Robert Richardson says in *Emerson: The Ideal in America,* "...was his effort to get it all into one statement, and he does in under a hundred pages. And it still has this electric jolt." Early on, he gives an account of one of those moments where the Ideal passes from the theoretical into actual experience, or rather he passes from the material into the Ideal.

> Crossing a bare common, in snow puddles, at twilight, under a clouded sky, without having in my thoughts any occurrence of special good fortune, I have enjoyed a perfect exhilaration. I am glad to the brink of fear. In the woods too, a man casts off his years, as the snake his slough, and at what period soever of life, is always a child. In the woods, is perpetual youth. Within these plantations of God, a decorum and sanctity reign, a perennial festival is dressed, and the guest sees not how he should tire of them in a thousand years. In the woods, we return to reason and faith. There I feel that nothing can befall me in life, -- no disgrace, no calamity, (leaving me my eyes,) which nature cannot repair. Standing on the bare ground, -- my head bathed by the blithe air, and uplifted into infinite space, -- all mean egotism vanishes. I become a transparent eye-ball; I am nothing; I see all; the currents of the Universal Being circulate through me; I am part or particle of God.

Later in it he devotes a chapter explicitly to *Idealism*, and the realm of "immortal necessary uncreated natures, that is, ... Ideas"

> As objects of science, they are accessible to few men. Yet all men are capable of being raised by

piety or by passion, into their region. And no man touches these divine natures, without becoming, in some degree, himself divine. Like a new soul, they renew the body. We become physically nimble and lightsome; we tread on air; life is no longer irksome, and we think it will never be so. No man fears age or misfortune or death, in their serene company, for he is transported out of the district of change. Whilst we behold unveiled the nature of Justice and Truth, we learn the difference between the absolute and the conditional or relative. We apprehend the absolute. As it were, for the first time, we exist. We become immortal, for we learn that time and space are relations of matter; that, with a perception of truth, or a virtuous will, they have no affinity.

Five years after *Nature,* in 1841, Emerson published the works for which he is still most known: the first series of *Essays.* It contains his most famous essay, *Self-Reliance,*[9] but also what I believe to be his clearest and most sustained explication and celebration of the Good, which he here calls *The Over-Soul:*

> The Supreme Critic on the errors of the past and the present, and the only prophet of that which must be, is that great nature in which we rest, as the earth lies in the soft arms of the atmosphere; that Unity, that Over-soul, within which every man's particular being is contained and made one with all other; that common heart, of which all sincere conversation is the worship, to which all right action is submission; that overpowering reality which confutes our tricks and talents, and

constrains every one to pass for what he is, and to speak from his character, and not from his tongue, and which evermore tends to pass into our thought and hand, and become wisdom, and virtue, and power, and beauty. We live in succession, in division, in parts, in particles. Meantime within man is the soul of the whole; the wise silence; the universal beauty, to which every part and particle is equally related; the eternal ONE. And this deep power in which we exist, and whose beatitude is all accessible to us, is not only self-sufficing and perfect in every hour, but the act of seeing and the thing seen, the seer and the spectacle, the subject and the object, are one. We see the world piece by piece, as the sun, the moon, the animal, the tree; but the whole, of which these are the shining parts, is the soul.

Near the end of the essay he counsels the need for the kind of stillness that echoes Ficino's admonition that "...we find eternal unity and the one eternity, not through movement or multiplicity, but through being still and being one."

Let man, then, learn the revelation of all nature and all thought to his heart; this, namely; that the Highest dwells with him; that the sources of nature are in his own mind, if the sentiment of duty is there. But if he would know what the great God speaketh, he must `go into his closet and shut the door,' as Jesus said. God will not make himself manifest to cowards. He must greatly listen to himself, withdrawing himself from all the accents of other men's devotion. Even their prayers are hurtful to him, until he have made his own. Our religion vulgarly stands on numbers of believers. Whenever the appeal is made -- no matter how indirectly -- to numbers, proclamation is then and there made, that religion is not. He that finds God a sweet, enveloping thought to him never counts his company. When I sit in that presence, who shall dare to come in? When I rest in perfect humility, when I burn with pure love, what can Calvin or Swedenborg say?

In a remarkable passage from *Self-Reliance* he speaks to our own ability to experience the Good; but that to know it, we must let go of all our preconceptions and our "passions" that keep us bound to the realm of the changeable.

And now at last the highest truth on this subject remains unsaid; probably cannot be said; for all that we say is the far-off remembering of the intuition. That thought, by what I can now nearest approach to say it, is this. When good is near you, when you have life in yourself, it is not by any known or accustomed way; you shall not discern the foot-prints of any other; you shall not see the face of man; you shall not hear any name;---- the way, the thought, the good, shall be wholly strange and new. It shall exclude example and experience. You take the way from man, not to man. All persons that ever existed are its forgotten ministers. Fear and hope are alike beneath it. There is somewhat low even in hope. In the hour of vision, there is nothing that can be called gratitude, nor properly joy. The soul raised over passion beholds identity and eternal causation, perceives the self-existence of Truth and Right, and calms itself with knowing that all things go well. Vast spaces of nature, the Atlantic Ocean, the South Sea, -- long intervals of time, years, centuries, -- are of no account. This which I think and feel underlay every former state of life and circumstances, as it does underlie my present, and what is called life, and what is called death.

[1]While I believe Emerson was a universal man, and that his revelations would have been the same wherever and whenever he appeared, there are key events in his life that I will be discussing. For more on this, there are biographies of course, the best of which is by Robert D. Richardson Jr., *Emerson: The Mind on Fire,* University of California Press, 1995. There is also my own video documentary, *Emerson: The Ideal in America.* (I will also just mention that I receive no income from the sale of these DVDs; all proceeds go to the RWE Institute.)

[2]The term Transcendentalist was originally applied to the group of German philosophers that included Kant, Hegel, Schelling and others, and this is as good a time as any to discuss why they are not included in this history. To be honest, I have not read them extensively, but I believe that their approach to the Ideal is that of the Sophists whom Socrates ridiculed; that is to say they make it a mental concept that can be described and debated, and their writing tends to obscure it. It becomes a subject for examination by the mind rather than the transcendent reality that produces the mind. I believe that reading any random paragraph of one of the Germans and one by any other the writers discussed here will reveal the difference in tone and understanding.

[3]I promise not to let the footnotes continue to be longer than the text, but I did just want to point out the missing sentence indicated by the ellipsis above as an example of Emerson's diving right into the subject. In one of the best summations I know of the Ideal he says, "The light is always identical in its composition, but it falls on a great variety of objects, and by so

falling is first revealed to us, not in its own form, for it is formless, but in theirs; in like manner, thought only appears in the objects it classifies."

4Robert D. Richardson Jr., *op. cit.* For more on MME, see Phyllis Cole, *Mary Moody Emerson and the Origins of Transcendentalism,* Oxford University Press, 1998

5Joel Porte, ed., *Emerson in His Journals,* Harvard University Press, 1982 All other journal quotes are from this source.

6Richardson, op. cit.

7In his journal on Aug. 27, 1836, Emerson says, "Today came to me the first proof-sheet of 'Nature' to be corrected, like a new coat, full of vexations; with the first sentences of the chapters perched like mottoes aloft in small type! The peace of the author cannot be wounded by such trifles, if he sees that the sentences are still good. A good sentence can never be put out of countenance by any blunder of compositors. It is good in text or note, in poetry or prose, as title or corollary. But a bad sentence shows all his flaws instantly by such dislocation." Joel Porte, ed., *op. Cit.*

8I also feel privileged and humbled. Quoting from Emerson is an embarrassment of riches; more a question of what to leave out than what to leave in. And at the same time he makes me want to be a better man, to realize my own "infinitude."

9This essay has had a long history of being read in a superficial way to encourage selfish behavior. As Robert Richardson has said, it is not about self-sufficiency but self-trust. Emerson himself was concerned in his own time as to how his words were being twisted, and in 1851, in his essay *The Fugitive Slave Law,* he states, "...self-reliance, the height and perfection of man, is reliance on God."

Chapter XIII: The Legacy of Transcendentalism

Transcendentalism and Spirituality

Many of the principles Americans take for granted can be traced to the "Transcendentalism" of Emerson and his circle, whether realized or not. In this chapter we will take a look at some of these principles and the people who helped to embed them into the modern American consciousness. The first, and perhaps most fundamental, is their insistence on the divine nature of each person, and its consequent effect on the expression of religion and spirituality.

In reading Emerson's ecstatic and blissful descriptions of the One, it's easy to forget that they were written against a backdrop of strong religious disagreements. The fracturing of the monolithic Christian church that had begun with Luther and led to the Pilgrims continued in the New World. In many ways, Boston, and Harvard in particular, were ground zero for much of this controversy. As Philip F. Gura makes clear in his book *American Transcendentalism: A History,* Harvard was in the thrall of German theology at this time: "...with the conclusion of the War of 1812 and the reopening of safe travel to Europe, Americans began to visit the Continent and to study at German universities. Among the most prominent of these pioneers were George Ticknor, Edward Everett, George Bancroft, and Frederic Henry Hedge, all of whom eventually carved out positions of intellectual leadership in New England and led efforts to disseminate German language and thought.[1]"

Although these men laid the groundwork from which New England Idealism could flower, eventually the turf wars being waged in German universities found their way to then New World as well and opened another front in their hairsplitting academic battles. Congregations underwent mitosis around the smallest points of doctrinal interpretation, losing sight of the overarching Christian principles of love and forgiveness.

Emerson, a Unitarian by training and by nature, was only too aware of the negative effects of this sectarianism, and it formed part of his decision to leave the ministry in 1831. In his journal on June 20 of that year he wrote, "Religion is the relation of the Soul to God, & therefore the progress of Sectarianism marks the decline of religion. For, looking at God instantly reduces our disposition to dissent from our brother. A man may die by fever as well as by consumption & religion is as effectually destroyed by bigotry as by indifference."

Especially after returning from Europe, Emerson had become a Protestant's protestant. His direct experiences of the Good, and his growing familiarity with the works of Plato and other non-Christian traditions, strengthened his belief in "the infinitude of the private man," but it also got him into hot water with the religious establishment of his day. What Kathleen Raine says of England--"It must also be remembered that the academic world at that time consisted of Protestant clergymen, to whom the Platonic theology must have been extremely distasteful[2]"--was also true of America. When Emerson made his points, during the Divinity School Address, about two defects of "historical Christianity," saying that they were preaching his story, not his message, and urged his listeners to "love God without mediator or veil," he was banned from speaking at Harvard for twenty years.

This view is also strongly expressed by other writers of the "Concord School". Henry David Thoreau saw the presence of an eternal intelligence amid the birth, growth, and decay of the natural world. In his attempt to "live deliberately," he moved, in 1845, into a cabin on Walden Pond (on land owned by Emerson), and took the natural world as his subject for study. He was perhaps our first Naturalist, but not of Nature per se. Through his patient observations, he reveals it not as something to be feared, conquered, or exploited, but as an ally in the process of spiritual awakening. In Walden he says, in a vivid reformulation of Plato's Divided Line, "As I stand over the insect crawling amid the pine needles on the forest floor, and endeavoring to conceal itself from my sight, and ask myself why it will cherish those humble thoughts, and hide its head from me who might perhaps be its benefactor, and impart to its race some cheering information, I am reminded of the greater Benefactor and Intelligence, that stands over me the human insect."

He sees being in nature as a way of forcing us to slow down, to connect with forces within that are deeper than the transitory thoughts that push and pull us each day. Also in Walden he says, "When we are unhurried and wise, we perceive that only great and worthy things have any permanent and absolute existence,--that petty fears and petty pleasures are but the shadow of the reality."

Walt Whitman, although not of Concord, embodied and expressed infinitude in a way that was often too much even for Emerson. But Emerson acknowledged that Whitman represented the kind of authentic, new American voice about which he had written so often. In 1855 he had received unannounced from Whitman his ambitious poem, "Leaves of Grass," and in a letter to a friend called it "the best piece of American Buddhism that anyone has had the strength to write, American to the bone." Whitman had returned the favor by saying "My ideas were simmering and simmering, and Emerson brought them to a boil." In a time when it seemed everyone wanted to be a poet, Whitman blew the roof off the poetry world by breaking just about every rule there was, starting with meter and rhyme.

Whitman's tone is that of the Creator himself taking endless delight in his own creation, seeing it all with equanimity and lack of judgment. From *Song of Myself*:

Trippers and askers surround me,
People I meet, the effect upon me of my early life or the ward and city I live in, or the nation,
The latest dates, discoveries, inventions, societies, authors old and new,
My dinner, dress, associates, looks, compliments, dues,

The real or fancied indifference of some man or
woman I love,
The sickness of one of my folks or of myself, or
ill-doing or loss or lack of money, or depressions
or exaltations,
Battles, the horrors of fratricidal war, the fever of
doubtful news, the fitful events;
These come to me days and nights and go from
me again,
But they are not the Me myself.
Apart from the pulling and hauling stands what I
am,
Stands amused, complacent, compassionating,
idle, unitary,
Looks down, is erect, or bends an arm on an
impalpable certain rest,
Looking with side-curved head curious what will
come next,
Both in and out of the game and watching and
wondering at it.
Backward I see in my own days where I sweated
through fog with linguists and contenders,
I have no mockings or arguments, I witness and
wait.[3]

So the God known to the Transcendentalists is
not the distant, severe God of the church
establishment: the Father-figure which uses fear and
the threat of punishment to control his "children." The
religious establishments are in the business of
providing identities to individuals: I am a Christian, I
am a Jew, I am a Muslim. But in doing so, they
prevent us from experiencing the Unity of the One;
they keep us in a state of duality, opposition,

alienation. This is fine for the ego--that which loves duality--but deadly for the soul.

For the Transcendentalists, God is the One, than which we cannot be other. It resists all attempts to define or limit. It is at the same time impersonal and totally personal--it is "the Me myself." It is that which has loved us since before we were born.

Another expression of it comes from the work of Jones Very, a mystic or madman or both, who was part of the Concord circle in the late 1830's. Although his poetry was diametrically opposed to Whitman's in style--he wrote in strict Shakespearean sonnet form-- his sense of the individual yet universal nature of this "Self" is the same.

The Better Self

I am thy other self, what thou wilt be,

When thou art I, the one seest now;

In finding thy true self thou wilt find me,

The springing blade, where now thou dost but plough.

I am thy neighbor, a new house I've built,

Which thou as yet hast never entered in;

I come to call thee; come in when thou wilt,

The feast is always ready to begin.

Thou should'st love me, as thou dost love thyself,

For I am but another self beside;

To show thee him thou lov'st in better health,

What thou would'st be, when thou to him hast died;

Then visit me, I make thee many a call;

Nor live I near to thee alone, but all.[4]

Transcendentalism and Education

Another area in which the influence of the Concord Idealists is still felt is that of education. The approach they brought to it is a logical outcome of the views we have seen regarding the soul; the self of each person and its immortality.

This in turn is derived from the view of Socrates, who of course also believed in the immortality of the soul. In *Meno* he attempts to demonstrate that at least some of the knowledge we exhibit in our lives comes from experiences we have had in previous ones, especially knowledge of virtues and the unchanging such as seen in mathematics.

> ...since the soul is immortal and often born, having seen what is on earth and within the house of Hades, and everything, there is nothing it has not learnt; so there is no wonder it can remember about virtue and other things, because it knew about these before. For since all nature is akin, and the soul had learnt everything, there is nothing to hinder a man, remembering one thing only--which men call learning--from himself finding out all else, if he is brave and does not

weary in seeking; for seeking and learning is all remembrance.[5]

Just as the the Idealists were consistent with this belief derived from Plato (and their own experience), it should be remembered that the state of education in the early 19th century was consistent with the prevailing Calvinist religious views of the time. This held that since humans were afflicted with original sin, children were even worse and had to be disciplined with corporal punishment: "Spare the rod and spoil he child." Teachers were expected to administer beatings as part of the job. Robert Richardson, in his biography of Henry David Thoreau, talks about Thoreau's first job after graduating from Harvard, in the Concord Public Schools: "A famous anecdote tells how one of the Concord school board members, Nehemiah Ball, went one day to observe Thoreau's teaching, called him into the hall, and reprimanded him for not using the cane. Stung and angered past self-possession, the impulsive twenty-year-old teacher went back into the classroom, picked out six students at random--rather as one deals with a mutiny in the army--and proceeded to beat them. He then quit the job. It was all terribly sudden. His entire career in the public schools was auspiciously launched and catastrophically concluded before a month had passed since commencement.[6]" If this was the case in "enlightened" Concord, one can only imagine conditions elsewhere.

Although there was an effort to make education universal, for most children subjects were limited to the very utilitarian--the three R's--and learning was done purely by rote. Classrooms were very spare and, especially in rural areas, children of different ages were all crammed together into the proverbial one-room schoolhouse. By contrast, the approach of the Idealists is summed up well in a passage from Emerson's essay, *Education*:

> I believe that our own experience instructs us that the secret of Education lies in respecting the pupil. It is not for you to choose what he shall know, what he shall do. It is chosen and foreordained, and he only holds the key to his own secret. By your tampering and thwarting and too much governing he may be hindered from his end and kept out of his own. Respect the child. Wait and see the new product of Nature. Nature loves analogies, but not repetitions. Respect the child. Be not too much his parent. Trespass not on his solitude.

The figures who were most central to the change from education by fear to education with love were Amos Bronson Alcott and Elizabeth Palmer Peabody, who for a time in the early 1830's collaborated in the experiment known as the Temple School.

Peabody was born into a prominent New England family, just about a year after Emerson's birth. She had two sisters who were also accomplished in their own right: Sophia was an artist who married Nathaniel Hawthorne and Mary Tyler, an author who shared Elizabeth's interest in childhood education and later married the educator Horace Mann. Elizabeth never married, and was in many ways a model for the independent woman of that time or any other. Among other ventures, she started a bookstore in Boston which became a salon and meeting-place for people interested in the "new ideas," and which also hostessed Margaret Fuller's "Conversations." She was also for a time the publisher of "The Dial," the circle's attempt at producing a magazine.

Bronson Alcott was born in 1799, and entirely self-educated. He was not born into the Concord circle but was adopted by it, especially Emerson, starting in 1835. His remarkable career of failures has been well-documented, and won't be repeated here, but his adherence to his own vision of the Ideal in the face of it is just as remarkable. Robert Richardson says of him, "Alcott now and for the rest of his life believed that the world of spirit is the only real world, and like William Blake he lived almost entirely in that world.[7]" He was apparently a remarkable presence and an entrancing speaker, but as was the case with Margaret Fuller ("My voice excites me; my pen never."), this did not translate into good writing. However, this does not seem to have concerned him in the least.[8]

Had he been a better writer, and also not so focused on children (still a good way to doom yourself to obscurity), he might have had an equal stature with Emerson and Thoreau. Now of course he is known mostly as the father of Louisa May Alcott. But reading the books which Elizabeth Peabody published as records of his methods at the Temple School, his approach still comes through as radical. He actually asks questions of the children, and then takes seriously their answers--especially on the subjects of God and the spirit (which of course would never be allowed today).

It would be rather easy to cherry-pick some quotes from these books as evidence of the remarkable insights the children can express when given the opportunity and the safe environment, but a real appreciation for his method comes only upon reading a number of the conversations. These are still most easily available in a reissue of Alcott's *Conversations with Children on the Gospels,* which was edited and reissued in 1991 by Alice O. Howell under the title *How Like an Angel Came I Down.* She offers this assessment of Alcott's work in her introduction:

> Alcott pioneered the idea of nonsectarian "spiritual culture" of children. We must not be deceived by the titles of his work into thinking that he was teaching Sunday School. He was not. He was applying a methodology of teaching used both by Socrates and Jesus Christ: the dialogue. For this Alcott was accused both of heresy and blasphemy. However, he was the first American teacher to have apprehended what Jung later was to call the "Collective Unconscious." "The world of the Spirit is the inward life of all things," is the way Alcott put it. And he felt that young children, not yet cut off, had ready access to it. For him, as for Wordsworth, the child came "trailing clouds of glory." Exposing them to those words of wisdom found in the works of the great philosophers and in the Gospels of the New Testament, he thought, would prove how we limit children by not grasping that the soul dwells, in part, always connected to the realm beyond time or space that we call eternity or what we recognize today as the unus mundus. [9]

It's unfortunate that sectarianism still prevails so completely that a school of this sort is difficult to imagine today, at least in the public sector. But the spirit of Alcott and Peabody and others who worked with them still comes through in the attempts by schools to accommodate and teach all children of different backgrounds and different capabilities. And even though educators are always under extreme pressure to teach only those things that can be readily tested and quantified, those who attempt to educe the spiritual qualities of compassion, creativity and self-realization are carrying on the work in which Alcott and Peabody labored in such obscurity.

Transcendentalism and Nature

One criticism that is sometimes leveled against Idealists is that they are neglectful of the physical world. Nature has, in fact, often been described as part of the spiritual problem, starting with Plato's Divided Line; not the ultimate illusion of reflection, but that which is reflected, still unreal in its own way. As with Aristophanes' caricature of Socrates in *The Clouds*,[10] Idealists are often seen as having their heads in, well, the clouds, without notice of or concern with the "real world." And it is true that pretty much all of the philosophers whom we've studied in this series lived in cities--Athens, Rome, Florence, London--and the world of nature does not play a large role in their writing.

At the same time, there is a long tradition of the retreat, if you will; of a place outside the city, more in touch with the natural world, a place of refuge and quiet which provides an environment amenable to the study of philosophy. Plato had his Academy in a grove of olive trees outside Athens, Plotinus his Campania, and Ficino his Careggi. Whether made explicit or not, they appreciated the renewing properties of nature while recognizing its limitations.

The connection does become explicit as Idealism moves into England and then America. Beginning, perhaps, with Wordsworth, there is a shift in the view of nature as something connected to a state of mind, something that can evoke thoughts and feelings when experienced and also when recollected. Remembering some beautiful scene from nature can help to bring one to that "inward eye / Which is the bliss of solitude...."

This theme of nature as a metaphor for the mind is elaborated upon clearly by Emerson in *Nature*, his first published work. To pick one passage, more or less at random:

> In the wilderness, I find something more dear and connate than in streets or villages. In the tranquil landscape, and especially in the distant line of the horizon, man beholds somewhat as beautiful as his own nature.
>
> The greatest delight which the fields and woods minister, is the suggestion of an occult relation between man and the vegetable. I am not alone and unacknowledged. They nod to me, and I to them. The waving of the boughs in the storm, is new to me and old. It takes me by surprise, and yet is not unknown. Its effect is like that of a higher thought or a better emotion coming over

me, when I deemed I was thinking justly or doing right.

Yet it is certain that the power to produce this delight, does not reside in nature, but in man, or in a harmony of both. It is necessary to use these pleasures with great temperance. For, nature is not always tricked in holiday attire, but the same scene which yesterday breathed perfume and glittered as for the frolic of the nymphs, is overspread with melancholy today. Nature always wears the colors of the spirit. To a man laboring under calamity, the heat of his own fire hath sadness in it. Then, there is a kind of contempt of the landscape felt by him who has just lost by death a dear friend. The sky is less grand as it shuts down over less worth in the population. (Chapter 1)

This view is noteworthy because the prevailing attitude was that of nature as a vast warehouse of raw materials to be exploited or a hostile force to be conquered. Nature was an "it," an "out there." When they looked at trees, men saw timber; when they looked at the landscape they saw farmfields. But just as the fate of their bodies was tied to nature, so was that of the mind: it brought about and reinforced the sense of duality, of alienation and materialism.

It's been said that the modern environmental movement was born on July 4, 1845, the day that Thoreau[11] took up residence in his cabin on Walden Pond. From this experience he produced his most famous work, although it was not published until almost ten years later, by which time he had again become a town-dweller. But both his "experiment" and the telling of it were unique in American letters at the time, and its place in them has grown greatly over time. It remains a manifesto for simple, non-materialistic living. He shared with Emerson the feeling of connection to nature: made of the same material, the same intelligence.

> The indescribable innocence and beneficence of Nature,--of sun and wind and rain, of summer and winter, -- such health, such cheer, they afford forever! and such sympathy have they ever with our race, that all Nature would be affected, and the sun's brightness fade, and the winds would sigh humanely, and the clouds rain tears, and the woods shed their leaves and put on mourning in midsummer, if any man should ever for a just cause grieve. Shall I not have intelligence with the earth? Am I not partly leaves and vegetable mould myself? (Walden, "Solitude")

This shift in viewpoint was made practical in the next generation in the person of John Muir, who was born in Scotland in 1838, two years after Emerson's *Nature* was published. He moved to America with his family when he was 11, and became as free a spirit as Thoreau ever was, living for a number of years in the Yosemite Valley. Emerson and Thoreau were inspirations to him, and he describes his meeting Emerson in 1871 this way:

> During my first years in the Sierra I was ever calling on everyone within reach to admire them (the forests of conifers), but I found no one half warm enough until Emerson came. I had read his essays, and felt sure that of all men he would best interpret the sayings of these noble mountains and trees. Nor was my faith weakened when I

met him in Yosemite. He seemed as serene as a Sequoia, his head in empyrean; and forgetting his age, plans, duties, ties of every sort, I proposed an immeasurable camping trip back in the heart of the mountains. He seemed anxious to go, but considerately mentioned his party.[12]

He acknowledges that Emerson was "too near the sundown of his life" at 68 (Muir was 33), and no doubt already exhibiting some of the dementia that would worsen until his death some 10 years later. But the baton had been passed--he says, "Emerson was still with me in spirit, though I never again saw him in the flesh. He sent books and wrote, cheering me on; advised me not to stay too long in solitude." Of course Muir, the archetypal mountain man, would go on to become the prototypical environmental lobbyist, advocating for the natural world through the intrigues of Washington DC, resulting in the formation of the National Park Service.

There is of course a kind of irony--or justice perhaps--in the fact that the reverence for the wild shown by Emerson, Thoreau and Muir (as well as many others) lives on because of their writing and publishing--one of the most civilized of human pursuits. All were voracious readers and prolific writers, and felt the need to share their experiences of solitude with the world. They all wrote movingly of the beauty of nature and the experience of a "transcendent" force when in its presence.

But my own feeling is that there is a subtle but profound difference in tone between Emerson and the others. They all see "God in Nature," in its lawfulness, beauty, and power, but to my ear Thoreau and Muir still see it as something "out there," still something separate, upon which they rely for an experience of beauty and harmony. Take away Nature and they are rather lost. In her essay, *Emerson and Thoreau as American Prophets of Eco-Wisdom,* Anne Woodlief says of Thoreau, "On the most transcendental level, though, he turned to nature for a beauty and harmony, even a civilized humanity, which he often found lacking in ordinary life, cherishing nature's 'eternal health' and 'perfect confidence.' Yet even in these moments he noted that he 'had seen into paradisaic regions' where he had 'hardly a foothold.'"[13] Compare this with Emerson's remark that, "Yet it is certain that the power to produce this delight, does not reside in nature, but in man, or in a harmony of both." There is not a separate beauty in the natural world; there is one beauty that permeates both the creation and man. Seeing the landscape "....man beholds somewhat as beautiful as his own nature."

This is, I submit, the beauty of the Good, the one true nature of us all, and recalls the teaching of Diotima from *The Symposium*:

> He who has been instructed thus far in the things of love, and who has learned to see the beautiful in due order and succession, when he comes toward the end will suddenly perceive a nature of wondrous beauty (and this, Socrates, is the final cause of all our former toils)—a nature which in the first place is everlasting, not growing and decaying, or waxing and waning; secondly, not fair in one point of view and foul in another, or at one time or in one relation or at one place

fair, at another time or in another relation or at another place foul, as if fair to some and foul to others, or in the likeness of a face or hands or any other part of the bodily frame, or in any form of speech or knowledge, or existing in any other being, as for example, in an animal, or in heaven, or in earth, or in any other place; but beauty absolute, separate, simple, and everlasting, which without diminution and without increase, or any change, is imparted to the ever-growing and perishing beauties of all other things.

Transcendentalism and Art

The last of the legacies of the Concord Idealists that we will consider is that if their impact on the artistic life of America and the world, specifically in the areas of poetry and music. And again, it pretty much all goes back to Emerson. His address to the Phi Beta Kappa Society of Harvard in 1837 has been called America's "Intellectual Declaration of Independence" by Oliver Wendell Holmes, and while it is aimed primarily at scholars, it also challenges artists to find their own connection to the Ideal and then create from it.

> Help must come from the bosom alone. The scholar is that man who must take up into himself all the ability of the time, all the contributions of the past, all the hopes of the future. He must be an university of knowledges. If there be one lesson more than another, which should pierce his ear, it is, The world is nothing, the man is all; in yourself is the law of all nature, and you know not yet how a globule of sap ascends; in yourself slumbers the whole of

Reason; it is for you to know all, it is for you to dare all.

Mr. President and Gentlemen, this confidence in the unsearched might of man belongs, by all motives, by all prophecy, by all preparation, to the American Scholar. We have listened too long to the courtly muses of Europe.

....A nation of men will for the first time exist, because each believes himself inspired by the Divine Soul which also inspires all men.

Emerson was, of course, a word man himself, and that is where his influence can be seen most clearly. He was a poet as well as an essayist, although it is ironic that in addition to quoting mostly Europeans in his essays, his verse is very traditionally structured in its meter and rhyme schemes. Even his poem *Threnody*, which is about the devastating loss of his young son Waldo, is very rigid in its meter and aabb rhyme scheme, as if he were trying to keep his emotions under control.

The theme of Man's divinity runs throughout his poetry, an early example being *Gnothi Seauton (Know Thyself)* from 1831, and we have already seen how the same theme is found in his contemporaries such as Jones Very and others. But Emerson's real legacy came in the person of Walt Whitman, who sent him an early copy of *Leaves of Grass* in 1855. Emerson's recognition was immediate--he knew this was the poet for whom he had been preparing the way, even though most people were shocked or stupefied by Whitman's work. Robert Richardson puts it this way:

For years Emerson was nearly alone in his admiration for Whitman. He was for Emerson the poet who had grasped more clearly than anyone else the idea that the poet is representative. Whitman was indeed the poet Emerson had called for in "the Poet," the person who claimed little or nothing for himself but got his material and his strength by acting as the conduit and spokesman--the representative--of everyone he had ever met or heard or read about.[14]

And Emerson's regard for Whitman was reciprocated. Richardson quotes from Horace Traubel's *With Walt Whitman in Camden:*

His usual manner carried with it something penetrating and sweet beyond description. There is in some men an indefinable something which flows out and over you like a flood of light--as if they possessed it illimitably--their whole being suffused with it. Being--in fact that is precisely the word. Emerson's whole attitude shed forth such an impression... Never a face more gifted with power to express, fascinate, maintain.[15]

It is also safe to say that another of Emerson's[16] legacies was Emily Dickinson, although of course he never got to read any of her poetry (hardly anyone did until after her death). But in her own way she also is a "representative poet," and one can imagine the other Transcendentalists smiling with approval at works such as this, her #76:

Exultation is the going

Of an inland soul to sea,

Past the houses--past the headlands--

Into deep Eternity--

Bred as we, among the mountains,

Can the sailor understand

The divine intoxication

Of the first league out from land?[17]

It is not, I think, hyperbole to say that all American poetry comes from these two streams: Whitman's roaring river and Dickinson's clear and gentle brook.

The influence of the Transcendentalists on music can be seen in that of Charles Ives. Although Ives was born in 1874, and so never met any of the Concord circle, he was intimately familiar with the spirit of their work as heard in his Piano Sonata #2. He obviously shared a common belief in the importance of revelation in the life of the artist, and had these experiences himself, as can be seen in this passage from his *Essays Before a Sonata*:[18]

> Emerson seems to use the great definite interests of humanity to express the greater, indefinite, spiritual values--to fulfill what he can in his realms of revelation. Thus, it seems that so close a relation exists between his content and expression, his substance and manner, that if he were more definite in the latter he would lose power in the former,--perhaps some of those occasional flashes would have been unexpressed--flashes that have gone down

through the world and will flame on through the ages--flashes that approach as near the Divine as Beethoven in his most inspired moments--flashes of transcendent beauty, of such universal import, that they may bring, of a sudden, some intimate personal experience, and produce the same indescribable effect that comes in rare instances, to men, from some common sensation.

In the early morning of a Memorial Day, a boy is awakened by martial music--a village band is marching down the street, and as the strains of Reeves' majestic Seventh Regiment March come nearer and nearer, he seems of a sudden translated--a moment of vivid power comes, a consciousness of material nobility, an exultant something gleaming with the possibilities of this life, an assurance that nothing is impossible, and that the whole world lies at his feet. But as the band turns the corner, at the soldiers' monument, and the march steps of the Grand Army become fainter and fainter, the boy's vision slowly vanishes--his"world" becomes less and less probable--but the experience ever lies within him in its reality.

Later in life, the same boy hears the Sabbath morning bell ringing out from the white steeple at the "Center," and as it draws him to it, through the autumn fields of sumac and asters, a Gospel hymn of simple devotion comes out to him--"There's a wideness in God's mercy"--an instant suggestion of that Memorial Day morning comes--but the moment is of deeper import-- there is no personal exultation--no intimate world vision--no magnified personal hope--and in their place a profound sense of a spiritual truth,--a sin within reach of forgiveness--and as the hymn voices die away, there lies at his feet-- not the world, but the figure of the Saviour--he sees an unfathomable courage, an immortality for the lowest, the vastness in humility, the kindness of the human heart, man's noblest strength, and he knows that God is nothing-- nothing but love!

Whence cometh the wonder of a moment? From sources we know not. But we do know that from obscurity, and from this higher Orpheus come measures of sphere melodies flowing in wild, native tones, ravaging the souls of men, flowing now with thousand-fold accompaniments and rich symphonies through all our hearts; modulating and divinely leading them.

As Whitman did with poetry, Ives took a look at the rulebook for music and casually tossed it over his shoulder. The range of expression in the Concord Sonata shows his understanding of the range of the Transcendentalists—from the wild dissonances of the Emerson movement to the comfortable homeiness of the Alcott. Also like Whitman he was a catalog, grabbing bits of folk tunes, college songs, Beethoven, and military marches, but still creating a unity from them. He can combine the raucous raging river of Whitman and the pure spring of Dickinson in the same piece. We may not "like" the result, but we know we are standing in the presence of someone who has heard the "melodies flowing in wild, native tones, ravaging the souls of men...."

The Ideal Today

What Emerson said at the beginning of *Nature* is still true for this age as well:

> Our age is retrospective. It builds the sepulchres of the fathers. It writes biographies, histories, and criticism. The foregoing generations beheld God and nature face to face; we, through their eyes. Why should not we also enjoy an original relation to the universe? Why should not we have a poetry and philosophy of insight and not of tradition, and a religion by revelation to us, and not the history of theirs? Embosomed for a season in nature, whose floods of life stream around and through us, and invite us by the powers they supply, to action proportioned to nature, why should we grope among the dry bones of the past, or put the living generation into masquerade out of its faded wardrobe? The sun shines to-day also. There is more wool and flax in the fields. There are new lands, new men, new thoughts. Let us demand our own works and laws and worship.

This is the irony of writing about the Ideal. All that is written about it confirms that it is infinite and everpresent, it exists now fully in each of us, no more or less than anyone whose words I have quoted. But we settle for quoting, for reading, for mere understanding. And I count myself in this group. We have many spiritual books (including this one) but how many true spirits? We have made a cottage industry of self-improvement, but we fail to see the Good, our real self, as unimprovable. As Plato says in *Phaedo*: "For 'many,' as they say in the mysteries, 'are the thyrsus bearers, but few are the mystics'—meaning, as I interpret the words, 'the true philosophers.'"

But we begin where we are, and if we stand in the company of these "true philosophers" as we have and as we will in the next section, we may perhaps join their company.

[1]Philip F. Gura, *American Transcendentalism: A History,* 2007, Hill and Wang, p. 26

[2]Kathleen Raine and George Mills Harper, eds., *Thomas Taylor the Platonist: Selected Writings*, Princeton University Press, 1969, p.21

[3]Allen Mandelbaum & Robert D. Richardson Jr., eds., *Three Centuries of American Poetry,* Bantam Books, 1999, p. 246

[4]Ibid., p. 212

[5]Plato, *The Meno,* from *The Complete Texts of Great Dialogues of Plato*, W.H.D. Rouse, trans., New American Library, 1970

[6]Robert D. Richardson Jr., *Henry Thoreau: A Life of the Mind*, University of California, 1986, p. 5

[7]Robert D. Richardson Jr., *Emerson: The Mind on Fire*, University of California, 1995, p. 212

[8]Thoreau says of Alcott in *Walden:* His words and attitude always suppose a better state of things than other men are acquainted with, and he will be the last man to be disappointed as the ages revolve. He has no venture in the present. But though comparatively disregarded now, when his day comes, laws unsuspected by most will take effect and masters of families and rulers will come to him for advice.--"How blind that cannot see serenity!

[9]A. Bronson Alcott, *How Like an Angel Came I Down,* edited by Alice O. Howell, Lindisfarne, 1991, p. xviii

[10]Aristophanes has Socrates say, "I have to suspend my brain and mingle the subtle essence of my mind with this air, which is of the like nature, in order clearly to penetrate the things of heaven. I should have discovered nothing, had I remained on the ground to consider from below the things that are above; for the earth by its force attracts the sap of the mind to itself. It's just the same with the watercress."

[11]Regarding the pronunciation of Thoreau's name, I offer this from the walden.org website, which corresponds to my own experience of how the Concordians pronounce it still: A note on pronouncing the name Thoreau: in determining the way in which to pronounce his name, it seems best to bow to the authority of those who knew the Thoreau Family well. Edward Emerson, the son of Ralph Waldo Emerson, is very clear. In a letter to Dr. Loring Holmes Dodd, October 11, 1918, he wrote: "We always called my friend Thó-row, the h sounded, and accent on the first syllable." [The Goddard Biblio Log, Spring 1973, p. 7]
[12]John Muir, *Forests of Yosemite Park,* from *John Muir: Nature Writings,* The Library of America, 1997, p. 786

[13]Anne Woodlief, *Emerson and Thoreau as American Prophets of Eco-wisdom,* online at http://www.vcu.edu/engweb/transcendentalism/criti cism/ecotran.html

[14]Robert D. Richardson Jr., *Emerson: The Mind on Fire,* University of California Press, 1995

[15]Ibid.

[16]Emerson's influence on literature still continues, of course, as can be seen in this quote about J. D. Salinger by Lillian Ross: Emerson was a touchstone, and Salinger often quoted him in letters. For instance, "A man must have aunts and cousins, must buy carrots and turnips, must have barn and woodshed, must go to market and to the blacksmith's shop, must saunter and sleep and be inferior and silly." Writers, he thought, had trouble abiding by that, and he referred to Flaubert and Kafka as "two other born non-buyers of carrots and turnips."

http://www.newyorker.com/talk/2010/02/08/100208ta_talk_ross#ixzz0fiqmUqlu

[17]Mandelbaum & Richardson, op. cit., p. 359

[18]Charles Ives, *Essays Before a Sonata,* Norton, 1961, p. 29 ff. Ives also has this to say about Emerson (p. 35):

> Perhaps, if all of Emerson--his works and his life--were to be swept away, and nothing of him but the record of the following incident remained to men--the influence of his soul would still be great. A working woman after coming from one of his lectures said: "I love to go to hear Emerson, not because I understand him, but because he looks as though he thought everybody was as good as he was." Is it not the courage--the spiritual hopefulness in his humility that makes this story possible and true? Is it not this trait in his character that sets him above all creeds--that gives him inspired belief in the common mind and soul? Is it not this courageous universalism

that gives conviction to his prophecy and that makes his symphonies of revelation begin and end with nothing but the strength and beauty of innate goodness in man, in Nature and in God, the greatest and most inspiring theme of Concord Transcendental Philosophy, as we hear it?

Part II: The Ideal as a Way of Life

Chapter XIV: A Natural History of the Ego

The Nature of the Ego

So if, as the Ideal tradition has taught us, the Good is the underlying Reality of all the phenomena we perceive, and if it is in fact our true nature, the reasonable question arises: why are we not in a state of full consciousness and bliss all the time? Why do we continue to live in the shadowland of the Cave when by rights we belong in the radiant sunshine outside it? Well, better pens than mine have attempted to answer this, so if you think you'll get a definitive answer here, you will probably be disappointed. But I may be able to offer some hints.

It really comes down to what we may call ego. This is not just ego in the sense of feeling self-important, or the Freudian sense of the arbiter between the id and superego, but any limitation put on the Good which prevents us from realizing it as our true nature. Emerson says, "The only sin is limitation." It can take the guise of self-pity, self-hatred, or just self-satisfaction, but it is a small, constrained sense of who we are. It is the source of all unhappiness, indecision, longing, attachment and fear. It it is immature, demanding, self-centered, and duplicitous, whether it is looking for praise or for pity. The ego is a sphincter on the soul.

This is certainly not to say that it resides equally in all people, and its negative effects are certainly more apparent in some than others, but the net effect

187

is to keep us from realizing our relationship to the Good, and with it our own true nature and potential. And unfortunately, it is scalable; the more efforts we make to realize the Good, the more efforts ego will make to prevent it.

I realize this is not an explanation, but the question of what ego is and where it comes from really only arises when we are not at one with the Good--the Good requires no explanations since it knows all, sees all and in fact creates all. Questions about the ego arise from the ego. Many attempts have been made to answer the question of why the limited world seems to exist using many different analogies; for example, it is all just a play (Maya) created by Absolute Consciousness for its own entertainment and enjoyment. God creates a perfect Eden, but Adam and Eve sin and are cast out of it. We drink from the river Lethe and forget (*aletheia*) the truth of our Being. But as long as the "explanations" are heard by the ego, they will be misunderstood--ego can "understand" only that which lies below it on the Divided Line, but not that "which passeth all understanding."

In fact the ego--and the world it creates-- is an illusion. We are never truly apart from the Good and can't be. But if the ego takes itself to be the true Self, it will project its own nature onto the world and see everything through its own darkened and distorted lens.

Essentially, this is the lens of duality. Me and everything else--all other people, all nature, all the manufactured world. Not to put too fine a point on it, it is a spoiled adolescent, a parasite—if we allow it to be. It is a necessary construction for living in the world of the mind, the way that the body is a construct for living in the world of matter. It goes, as they say, with the territory. But ego cannot see that it is a part of and player in the world. That would in a real sense destroy it, and it will do anything for self-preservation. So it maintains a variety of strategies to keep us thinking that it is in fact who we are, and it will be some of these strategies--the nature of the ego--that we will consider in this chapter. These strategies are all interconnected, and if we can start to observe some of them, we can start to see through them and realize our connection to the Good.

The purpose of the soul is to unite; the purpose of the ego is to divide and multiply. It starts by creating two—me and everything else—and then goes on to create thousands, millions. And the next act of the ego, which happens seemingly in a nanosecond, is to find someone to whom to feel superior. The mechanism for maintaining this feeling is the everyday mechanical mind, which delights in making endless microjudgments about whomever or whatever it sees. Me vs. them. My gene pool, gender, race, party, belief system, team, country, and especially my religion. The Good is self-sufficient and constant; the ego is addicted to novelty and craves "insider information," "exclusive offers," gossip, occult knowledge, secret powers; anything to make it feel special and superior. Perhaps most especially, great wealth, the desire to have "more money than God." It is well to remember that God has no money.

After limiting our consciousness, ego goes on to make itself the center of our attention, and it does this by assuming any role necessary. It can go from feeling practically all-powerful to feeling practically worthless in a matter of seconds. As required it can be charming, boring, judgmental, accepting, aggressive, passive, selfish, generous. If it feels itself to be weak and not interesting, it can become fascinated by other people's egos and the cult of celebrity, in which the work or the creation is the byproduct, and self-promotion is the main thing. It seems to come with a set of likes and dislikes, characteristics and opinions, that are never really examined, just accepted. We are "born this way," and that's enough. Any questioning is done within the confines of the closed system of the ego, which cannot see anything except itself.

Another tool the ego uses to keep us limited is what has been called the stream of consciousness, the endless monologue flowing in our heads. The Good is truly the Ocean of Consciousness, the infinite and unchanging Sea of Love; ego changes from being a babbling brook to a churning muddy river full of uprooted trees and dead cows. The ocean is its source, but as it is with a physical river its quality and nature can vary wildly. The more we realize that this stream does not come from us, the more we can appreciate the source of the water itself. As Emerson says in The Over-Soul, "When I watch that flowing river, which, out of regions I see not, pour for a season its streams into me, I see that I am a pensioner; not a cause, but a surprised spectator of this ethereal water; that I desire and look up, and put myself in the attitude of reception, but from some alien energy the visions come."

Emerson speaks here also to another strategy of the ego: claiming. Most of us will look at that flowing river and think we own it. The artist who taps into it as the source of inspiration, the unhappy person who sees it as the source of her bad luck, the timid person afraid to take too much--all are claiming it as their own in a way. What it brings is matched to our expectations of it, and we feel that, good or bad, we deserve whatever it brings. But this water belongs to no one, is freely given and inexhaustible. We have no right to it, but it is ours as long as we don't try to possess it. For those who do, there is a price to be paid.

When the source is claimed and limited in this way, the mind and the emotions become purely mechanical. The mind becomes like an asteroid belt beyond which our spiritual consciousness cannot penetrate. It creates the boundaries of who we think we are. Similarly with the emotions—we are reduced to the Pavlovian model of stimulus and response. Someone pushes a certain emotional button and we react in a predictable way, especially when it comes to the negative feelings. In fact we are no more these feelings that we are our bodies. But while we are accustomed to speaking of the body in the third person—"I have a pain in my back"—we speak of transient ideas or emotions as if they were us. Rather than "I am angry," saying "I have an inflammation in my anger plexus," would make more sense, and make us want to treat it, not prolong it.

It is desire, not love, that makes the world go 'round. Love makes the world fall still. In the Good, love is only emotion, but all negative emotions spring from the ego, and it delights in wallowing in them. Hatred is love perverted, greed is abundance made personal. How many relationships have been destroyed because someone said something about someone and both are too proud to apologize or forgive? How big a bag of anger, hurt, resentment, fear and duplicity do we carry around? How readily can we still "pull the files" on events that happened long ago, and go over them in detail, perhaps rewriting them with stronger adjectives, more conflict, greater outrage?

This speaks to another tendency of the ego: pulling the mind into the past or the future. The Good is known in what has been called the eternal now, in all its perfection. The ego would have us dwell in the past or anticipate a future which will be better, always existing in a state of dissatisfaction, and blaming circumstances or other people for it, living a life as Thoreau said of "quiet desperation."

What is the remedy? For starters we can learn to examine all our thoughts and actions for signs of duplicity. Saying something about someone in an email that you don't want them to see can and probably will come back to haunt you. Thinking your life would be better if only you had this or that, him or her. Reliving the pains of the past. When these are seen, to start to bring desires, thoughts, words and actions into alignment, with nothing hidden. To become like the sun, radiating warmth and light constantly and in all directions. To remember the words of Ficino:

> Then let us not be moved or distracted by many things, but let us remain in unity as much as we are able, since we find eternal unity and the one eternity, not through movement or multiplicity, but through being still and being one.[1]

Another way the ego limits us is by determining our attitudes towards "religion"--one of the first ways being to create a separate category of experience called "religion." In the ancient Greek philosophical schools, there was no distinction made between life and philosophy--as summed up in the title of Pierre Hadot's excellent book on the subject, they viewed "Philosophy As a Way of Life." It was not a purely academic study the way it is treated now, which allows you to study and debate ethics endlessly, and then still go out and perform harmful actions without fear of contradiction. Religion generally requires a higher standard of behavior, but it is still something that can be divorced from our lives by performing certain rituals on a regularly scheduled basis.

The kind of religion usually practiced by the ego takes a similar form regardless of the name it goes by. In all cases it is authoritarian: God is an all-powerful and rather capricious father figure "out there" somewhere, who has an insatiable need to be worshiped and whose main goal seems to be to keep me from having a good time by employing a system of rewards and punishments. What I enjoy is a sin and I will be punished for doing it; what I don't enjoy God does and will reward me for doing it. God's real ace in the hole in this system is the final judgment--I can enjoy myself on earth, but after death I will pay for it by being consigned to eternal damnation.

Given its essentially adolescent nature, this is of course exactly what we could predict that the ego would believe. In this view, God is kind of an ego-in-chief, an "alpha ego" to which ours can aspire as a model of self-absorption. It is the view often held by religious fundamentalists of all stripes, and helps justify their own need for power, a sense of superiority, hatred of the infidel, and devotion to a mission. It is a view that is very useful for keeping the established power structure in power. But it's not just believers who become attached to this perspective-- atheistic egos also often invoke it when arguing against the existence or legitimacy of such a Supreme Being.

If you've read this far, you know that this in no way corresponds to the way the Good is represented by Plato or any of the other Idealists we've considered. In Plato's description of "The Child of the Good:"

Now, that which imparts truth to the known and the power of knowing to the knower is what I would have you term the idea of good, and this you will deem to be the cause of science, and of truth in so far as the latter becomes the subject of knowledge; beautiful too, as are both truth and knowledge, you will be right in esteeming this other nature as more beautiful than either; and, as in the previous instance, light and sight may be truly said to be like the sun, and yet not to be the sun, so in this other sphere, science and truth may be deemed to be like the good, but not the good; the good has a place of honour yet higher.

The emphasis here is on "truth and beauty," on light and on reason. This theme runs throughout the descriptions by other writers we've studied, from Plotinus' "The One" to Emerson's "The Over-Soul." To be fair, there are of course people in all the major (and minor) religions who are not authoritarian in their approach. And also to be fair, Plato does give a narrative of a judgment after death in the Myth of Er, in the last book of the Republic, but in it the deceased pass judgment on themselves by choosing another life into which to be reborn. So in the Ideal tradition, there is no reward and punishment per se--any suffering we experience is a result of our being separated from the light, from the Good which is our true nature. The "sins" we commit are the thoughts, feelings and actions that perpetuate this separation-- we trade the bliss of being with the One for winning the little prizes of the prisoners in the cave.[2] When we shed the limiting ego, and experience that light within, we become as gods ourselves.

I think it would be helpful to examine these different conceptions through the use of two works of art, both created in the Renaissance. (Islam has its own version of the Day of Judgment, but of course no graphical representations of it.

The first is a fairly traditional rendering from the Chronicles of Nuremberg (1493) of the official version of the Last Judgment, as found in the Book of Matthew, Chapter 25, which theme has been rendered by any number of artists over the years. It shows

Christ, the largest, hence most important figure, seated on a heavenly throne surrounded by angels and saints, passing judgment on the people of the earth, and casting the sinners into the eternal damnation beneath it. The naked (they're almost always naked) damned, are seen tumbling into hell to be devoured by beasts and endure other tortures[2], which process is being overseen by the Archangel Michael wielding his sword.

While I don't wish to give offense, it appears to me that the image and the conception behind it are ones of division and fear. ("Well, duh," I hear you say.) But the Good is antithetical to fear, and nothing good comes from fear. It brings to mind another quote from Emerson regarding the use of punishment in dealing with his young son: If I am wilful, he sets his will against mine, one for one, and leaves me, if I please, the degradation of beating him by my superiority of strength. But if I renounce my will, and act for the soul, setting that up as umpire between us two, out of his young eyes looks the same soul; he reveres and loves with me. *(The Over-Soul)*

"The Last Judgment," from the Nuremberg Chronicles

"The Liberation of St. Peter," by Raphael Sanzio, 1514

Contrast this with another painting in the remarkable collection of wall paintings known as the Raphael Rooms in the Vatican. (These are the same rooms which house the ubiquitous "School of Athens," which we discussed previously, and which of course shows his familiarity with the Ideal tradition.) This painting depicts "The Liberation of St. Peter" from prison, as recounted in Acts 12:3–19. King Herod has imprisoned Peter, but at night an angel comes and liberates him from his chains and releases him from the cell while the guards sleep.

The parallels between this and the Cave Allegory are striking. Like the prisoners in the cave, Peter is bound by chains. Unconsciousness prevails--the guards are asleep, their faces hidden, and so is Peter in the cell. The only light in the scene is firelight, as in the cave, or the reflected light of the moon--until, that is, the angel arrives, being its own source of light.

Then the angel leads Peter by the hand out of the cell past the sleeping guards. There is none of the cinematic suffering and violence of the crucifixion or the Last Judgment. It is almost boring in its ordinariness--man is in prison, but following the light frees him from it--which is no doubt one of the reasons why it lost out.

So unlike the image of judgment and punishment, this can serve as an analogy for how the Good works to bring about our "salvation." As Plato sums it up in speaking of the cave:

This entire allegory, I said, you may now append, dear Glaucon, to the previous argument; the prison-house is the world of sight, the light of the fire is the sun, and you will not misapprehend me if you interpret the journey upwards to be the ascent of the soul into the intellectual world according to my poor belief, which, at your desire, I have expressed whether rightly or wrongly God knows. But, whether true or false, my opinion is that in the world of knowledge the idea of good appears last of all, and is seen only with an effort; and, when seen, is also inferred to be the universal author of all things beautiful and right, parent of light and of the lord of light in this visible world, and the immediate source of reason and truth in the intellectual; and that this is the power upon which he who would act rationally, either in public or private life must have his eye fixed.

By the same token, we are not rewarded for our good behavior either. When we stop seeing the world through the dualistic lens of the ego, when we stop thinking of ourselves as separate, when we realize that our essential nature is in fact the same as that of the Good, we can say with Emerson in *Nature*, "--all mean egotism vanishes. I become a transparent eyeball; I am nothing; I see all; the currents of the Universal Being circulate through me; I am part or parcel of God. ....I am the lover of uncontained and immortal beauty."

The History of the Ego

We have looked at the nature of the ego as part of our natural history, so now it just remains to look at its history; that is, how it has been represented in art and literature over the ages.

This struggle between what may be called the soul and the ego is one of the most enduring themes of all eras and cultures. It is embodied in our most ancient myths, whether explicitly or symbolically. In all cultures there are stories of a Golden Age of harmony when people were in touch with their true Good-like nature, often represented by some magical object. But then something happens; some new alien force--the ego--enters, and the Good is lost, stolen, usurped, forgotten, ignored, imprisoned, banished, attenuated, fallen, attached, hypnotized, dormant, covered, darkened, limited, exiled, ostracized, displaced, or ensnared. This is the separation phase of the *monomyth*, as we have previously discussed. As described by Joseph Campbell, what happens next is:

A hero ventures forth from the world of the common day into a region of supernatural wonder: fabulous forces are there encountered and a decisive victory is won: the hero comes back from this mysterious adventure with the power to bestow boons on his fellow man.[3]

In short, he regains his own soul. Campbell goes on to give a number of examples of the basic theme: Prometheus and fire. Jason and the Golden Fleece. Aeneas in the Underworld. Gautama's transformation into the Buddha. All the quest stories can be seen as the struggle by which the soul/hero reclaims its true nature from the ego/usurper. So add to this list the Iliad, the Odyssey, the Bhagavad Gita, the Grail, Frodo and the Ring, and particularly stories of slaying the dragon. Again, to quote Joseph Campbell, in his conversation with Bill Moyers, published as *The Power of Myth*[4]:

> Psychologically, the dragon is one's own binding of oneself to one's ego. We're captured in our own dragon cage. ....The ultimate dragon is within you, it is your ego clamping you down.

And he goes on to say how in Western myths the dragon "tries to collect and keep everything to himself. In his secret cave he guards things: heaps of gold and perhaps a captured virgin. He doesn't know what to do with either, so he just guards and keeps."

Sound familiar?

So the "fictional" ego has been with us forever; the more "philosophical" almost as long. While Plato didn't use a specific term like "ego," he discusses in a number of dialogs the effect on the man who identifies with the body and is pulled into the world of appearances and desires by it. The most extensive description occurs in books 8 and 9 of *The Republic*, as Plato discusses the four different kinds of states and the individual personalities that correspond to them. These are Timocratic man who desires honor and glory, the Oligarchic man who desires money at all costs, the Democratic man who values liberty above all, and the Tyrannical man who is single-minded in pursuing his own thirst for power and control. As Plato describes them, some are worse than others, but all are devoted to their own ends at the expense of the whole state, the unity. The tyrant of course is the worst-- he has no redeeming qualities, and everything said about it can apply to the ego--our own resident Muammar Qaddafi. Plato sums up his discussion giving a hypothetical dialog with a man who would give up his Goodly nature for some perceived transitory benefit:

> Socrates: Come, now, and let us gently reason with the unjust, who is not intentionally in error. 'Sweet Sir,' we will say to him, what think you of things esteemed noble and ignoble? Is not the noble that which subjects the beast to the man, or rather to the god in man; and the ignoble that which subjects the man to the beast?' He can hardly avoid saying yes --can he now?
>
> Glaucon: Not if he has any regard for my opinion.
>
> Socrates: But, if he agree so far, we may ask him to answer another question: 'Then how would a man profit if he received gold and silver on the condition that he was to enslave the noblest part of him to the worst? Who can imagine that a man who sold his son or daughter into slavery for money, especially if he sold them into the hands of fierce and evil men, would be the gainer, however large might be the sum which he

received? And will any one say that he is not a miserable caitiff who remorselessly sells his own divine being to that which is most godless and detestable?"

This is very similar, of course, to the later saying of Jesus in Mark 8:36, "For what shall it profit a man, if he shall gain the whole world, and lose his own soul?"

Another vivid description of the ego comes from the writings Hermes Trismegistus. I've avoided including him thus far because his place in the Ideal tradition is not as easily determined as others we have discussed. When his writings first appeared in the West in the Renaissance (and translated also by Ficino) he was originally thought to be contemporaneous with Moses, Egyptian in origin, and a lawgiver to both Eastern and Western traditions. His dates were later revised to post-Plato, and probably pre-Plotinus, although no one seems to be able to put him in a precise period. I for one see enough similarity of ideas and imagery to believe that he is part of the tradition. In any case, he delivers the following admonition to those who wish to return to the Good, but are living under the tyranny of the ego:

> But first you must rip off the tunic that you wear, the garment of ignorance, the foundation of vice, the bonds of corruption, the dark cage, the living death, the sentient corpse, the portable tomb, the resident thief, the one who hates through what he loves and envies through what he hates. Such is the odious tunic you have put on. It strangles you and drags you down with it so that you will not hate its viciousness, not look up and see the fair

vision of truth and the good that lies within, not understand the plot that it has plotted against you when it made insensible the organs of sense, made them inapparent and unrecognized for what they are, blocked up with a great load of matter and jammed full of loathsome pleasure, so that you do not hear what you must hear nor observe what you must observe.[5]

No "sweet sir," here. "The portable tomb, the resident thief." That about says it all.

Plotinus, the advocate for the One, also realized that there was some "other" that somehow makes us forget the One. He too invokes the image of a human as a microcosm of the state, and associates our "becom(ing) a dual thing" with an attachment to the body.

Even now, it is true, we are not put apart; but upon that Primal man there has intruded another, a man seeking to come into being and finding us there, for we were not outside of the universe. The other has wound himself about us, foisting himself upon the Man that each of us was at first. Then it was as if one voice sounded, one word was uttered, and from every side an ear attended and received and there was an effective hearing, possessed through and through of what was present and active upon it: now we have lost that first simplicity; we are become the dual thing, sometimes indeed no more than that later foisting, with the primal nature dormant and in a sense no longer present ...
This is the evil of state and of council: and this is the evil of man; man includes an inner rabble--pleasures,

desires, fears--and these become masters when the man, the manifold, gives them play. But one that has reduced his rabble and gone back to the Man he was, lives to that and is that Man again, so that what he allows to the body is allowed as to something separate.[6]

We see again here the important distinction, as we discussed in the last chapter, between the philosophical approach to the ego expressed here, and the religious view of reward and punishment. We are not "bad" because we have an ego, just mistaken. We are victims of the "inner rabble--pleasures, desires, fears--" and have only to reduce our rabble to return to our primal state, the One.

I was going to write another chapter on the ego, but then decided it would be giving it too much attention, which is of course exactly what it wants. So enough. You get the idea. All the adjectives you use to describe yourself--male, female, black, white, gay, straight, success, failure, old, young--are all just properties of your body, your mind or your emotions. They are not, as Whitman said, "the Me Myself." They are things you have, not what you are. So have them, but don't be had by them. Embark on your quest. Bust the thief, slay the dragon. Be your own hero.

[1]Marsilio Ficino, *Meditations on the Soul,* translated by members of the Language Department of the School of Economic Science, London, Clement Salaman, ed. Inner Traditions, 1996

[2]And if they were in the habit of conferring honours among themselves on those who were quickest to observe the passing shadows and to remark which of them went before, and which followed after, and which were together; and who were therefore best able to draw conclusions as to the future, do you think that he would care for such honours and glories, or envy the possessors of them? Would he not say with Homer: Better to be the poor servant of a poor master, and to endure anything, rather than think as they do and live after their manner? *Plato, The Republic*

[3]Joseph Campbell, *The Hero with a Thousand Faces*, Princeton University Press, 1968, p. 30

[4]Joseph Campbell, *The Power of Myth,* Doubleday, 1988, p. 149

[5]Brian P. Copenhaver, trans., *Hermetica*, Cambridge, 1992, p. 24

[6]Plotinus, *The Enneads,* translated by Stephen McKenna, Penguin, 1991, p. 453-4

Chapter XV: The Ideal and the Art of Dying

"...that those who apply themselves correctly to the pursuit of philosophy are in fact practicing nothing more nor less than death and dying." Plato, "Phaedo"[1]

The nature of death is one of the great philosophical questions, right up there with "What am I?" What is death? Does something survive the death of the body? This question, explicitly or implicitly, with its hope for or fear of survival, permeates all cultures and gives rise to their deepest myths and rituals. And yet most people seem to live their lives without regard to death except for a vague fear, kicking it down the road until they are told that they have x months to live. Better late than never, perhaps, but I wish to argue, with Plato, that an understanding of death can be an excellent guide in knowing how to live. We spend so much of our time and attention dealing with ephemera, or trying to keep ourselves entertained or distracted, that the appearance of the prospect of our own death or that of someone we love can automatically give us a larger perspective and a reason to think about what is important, what lasts, why we are here.

I hope it is immediately apparent that seen through the lens of the Ideal that the subject is not morbid, frightening, depressing or even particularly fascinating. It has nothing to do with the current preoccupation with the supernatural or zombies (except insofar as they are symbols of the "waking sleep" in which we spend most of our lives).

"Practicing...death and dying" is not the same as being preoccupied with it, or wishing for it, or fearing it. But it is one of the most important things we humans face in any age, and I believe it is especially important to come to terms with it in an age where medicine can keep a heartbeat going almost indefinitely and treats death as a failure. We need to acknowledge that at some point, our bodies, and all we have invested in them, will cease to function. We need to realize that, according to Idealism, death is a blip in consciousness. We need to realize with a prominent contemporary Idealist, Eckhart Tolle, that "Death is not the opposite of life. Life has no opposite. The opposite of death is birth. Life is eternal."[2]

So in this next chapter, we'll be looking at what Idealism has to say about death, and in particular, this question of the immortality of the soul. We will begin with Plato, for whom the question became central after he did see someone he loved--Socrates--executed in 399 BC. He treats the subject in a number of dialogues, but perhaps most thoroughly in the *Phaedo,* which "records" the conversation of Socrates and some his followers on the day he dies.[3] In many ways it is a condensed version of Plato's thought, with a brief overview of the Ideal Forms, instruction in the virtuous life, some cosmology and a tour of the Underworld.

Plato assumes the existence of the soul, and much of the dialogue concerns itself with a "proof" of the soul's immortality, which I will not attempt to summarize here; it will not persuade any "sensible" person. But it is consistent with and central to

Socrates' Theory of Forms: that there are eternalities of which the things in the visible realm are just instances in time and space. The soul is distinct from the body, and it does survive when the body dies, in the same way that Beauty survives when an individual flower dies. The soul exists before it becomes affiliated with the body in this life, wears it like a suit of clothes, and continues to exist after the body falls away. This conviction is at the heart of Socrates' calmness in the face of his impending execution.

> Then, Simmias, as the true philosophers are ever studying death, to them, of all men, death is the least terrible. Look at the matter in this way: how inconsistent of them to have been always enemies of the body, and wanting to have the soul alone, and when this is granted to them, to be trembling and repining; instead of rejoicing at their departing to that place where, when they arrive, they hope to gain that which in life they loved (and this was wisdom), and at the same time to be rid of the company of their enemy.

Socrates is rather hard on the body in this dialogue, not just because he sees its appetites for "so-called pleasures," but also since

> ... the body is a source of endless trouble to us by reason of the mere requirement of food; and also liable to diseases which overtake and impede us in the search after truth: and by filling us so full of loves, and lusts, and fears, and fancies, and idols, and every sort of folly, prevents our ever having, as people say, so much as a thought. For whence come wars, and fightings, and factions? whence but from the body and the lusts of the body? For wars are occasioned by the love of

money, and money has to be acquired for the sake and in the service of the body; and in consequence of all these things the time which ought to be given to philosophy is lost.[4]

So for Plato there is never any real question but that the soul is immortal. "That soul, I say, herself invisible, departs to the invisible world, to the divine and immortal and rational: thither arriving, she lives in bliss and is released from the error and folly of men, their fears and wild passions and all other human ills, and forever dwells, as they say of the initiated, in company with the gods."

And the same can be said for Marsilio Ficino. His magnum opus, *The Platonic Theology*[5] (subtitled *On the Immortality of the Soul)*, which runs to 18 books, (and which shows that like Plotinus he has a rather mind-numbingly pedantic side), is his own attempt at a proof, and as we saw earlier, it is generally acknowledged that it was he who made immortality part of the Catholic doctrine. But the standard Christian view is that the soul is immortal in one direction only--it is somehow born with the body, and then "achieves" immortality through its belief in and forgiveness by Jesus Christ. I think it is safe to say this was not Ficino's view. In the introduction to *The Platonic Theology,* Michael Allen and James Hankins say "...he believed, with St. Augustine, not only will the soul achieve immortality, but that it is intrinsically and everlasting immortal, immortal from its creation, and therefore by nature angelic, divine, made in the image and likeness of the eternal."[6] Any notion of limitation, of time or space, comes from the ego, which will persist in trying to convince you that you are limited until you have the actual experience, before death or after it, that you are not.

So immortality is not being everlasting; it is being everpresent. We should neither hope for nor fear the inevitable future, but make ourselves unburdened and worthy at each moment. As Emerson, from whom we will hear much more in the next section, says in his essay *Worship:*

> Of immortality, the soul, when well employed, is incurious. It is so well, that it is sure it will be well. It asks no questions of the Supreme Power. The son of Antiochus asked his father, when he would join battle? "Dost thou fear," replied the King, "that thou only in all the army wilt not hear the trumpet?" 'Tis a higher thing to confide, that, if it is best we should live, we shall live, — 'tis higher to have this conviction, than to have the lease of indefinite centuries and millenniums and aeons. Higher than the question of our duration is the question of our deserving. Immortality will come to such as are fit for it, and he who would be a great soul in future, must be a great soul now. It is a doctrine too great to rest on any legend, that is, on any man's experience but our own. It must be proved, if at all, from our own activity and designs, which imply an interminable future for their play.[7]

That We Do Not Have a Right to the People We Love

One of the characteristics of the Idealists we've studied is that for the most part they are not ascetics, withdrawing from the world to seek unity (not that there's anything wrong with that). While Plato,

Plotinus and Ficino never married or had children, they did have a large and active circle of friends and worldly responsibilities. Socrates, Taylor and Emerson had wives and children, although in the case of Socrates it could be said that his students were his real children. In short, they all were surrounded by people they loved, and who loved them, and they experienced the death of some they loved. How they handled these deaths says a lot about them, and about the Ideal from which they drew their strength.

The death of Socrates has of course become the stuff of myth. We have already quoted extensively from Plato's account of his death in the *Phaedo*, and it is evident that he did not fear death, consistent with his expressed belief in the immortality of his soul. But it is the very human reactions of the disciples in his cell that evoke the sympathy of those of us who are disciples after 2500 years. He has "convinced" us all that "Then, Cebes, beyond question, the soul is immortal and imperishable, and our souls will truly exist in another world!" And yet when the poison is spreading through his body and he remains calm and still, the disciples break down in grief anyway.

> And hitherto most of us had been able to control our sorrow; but now when we saw him drinking, and saw too that he had finished the draught, we could no longer forbear, and in spite of myself my own tears were flowing fast; so that I covered my face and wept, not for him, but at the thought of my own calamity in having to part from such a friend.

That's really the crux of it, isn't it? Based on what Socrates has taught, there should be rejoicing in the cell, but we weep; we weep for ourselves, for our own loss, our own deprivation, our own calamity. We know the world is transient, but we wish it to endure; we know that everything and everyone in it is leased, but we wish to possess. Learning that we do not have a right to those we love, that in believing so we limit ourselves and the loved one, is one of the most profound lessons we can learn from philosophy.

There is perhaps no better example of one who did learn this lesson than Emerson. Long-lived himself (he died at 79), he experienced many premature deaths, starting with three siblings who died in childhood, and his father who died when Waldo was eight. Two other brothers, Edward and Charles, with whom he was very close, died a couple of years apart in their twenties. But none of these deaths in his early years affected him as deeply as did that of his first wife Ellen Louisa Tucker.

Emerson had met her while preaching in Concord, New Hampshire when he was 24 and she was 17. They were married in 1829. Emerson had been appointed to be pastor of the Second Church of Boston, a prestigious position that also brought him more money than he had ever known. He was on his way to being a respected and respectable minister like his father. Ellen was delicate and already suffering from tuberculosis, but they both prayed that she would be cured. When she died on February 8 1831, Emerson went numb. Five days later, writing in his journal, the entry is painful to read.

Never any one spake with greater simplicity or cheerfulness of dying. She said, "'I pray for sincerity & that I may not talk, but may realize what I say." She did not think she had a wish to get well, & told me "she would do me more good by going than by staying; she should go first & explore the way, & comfort me." ....One of the last things she said after much rambling and inarticulate expression was "I have not forgot the peace & joy." And at nine o'clock she died. Farewell blessed spirit who hast made me happy in thy life & in thy death make me yet happy in thy disembodied state.[8]

The passage in its entirety represents a struggle between his wanting to hold onto her and his realization that she had her own mission to fulfill. He grieved, obviously, but he is remarkably free of self-pity, anger, or bitterness. He continued to address her in his journals, and as time went on he seems to have realized that her death was meant to free him from the path of convention and respectability on which he had embarked. Ten years later, in his essay *Compensation*, he wrote:

And yet the compensations of calamity are made apparent to the understanding also, after long intervals of time. A fever, a mutilation, a cruel disappointment, a loss of wealth, a loss of friends, seems at the moment unpaid loss, and unpayable. But the sure years reveal the deep remedial force that underlies all facts. The death of a dear friend, wife, brother, lover, which seemed nothing but privation, somewhat later assumes the aspect of a guide or genius; for it commonly operates revolutions in our way of life, terminates an epoch of infancy or of youth which was waiting to be closed, breaks up a wonted occupation, or a household, or style of living, and allows the formation of new ones more friendly to the growth of character.

So death is not a loss to the one who dies, and it need not be a loss to the ones who live. In everyone's life there seems to be someone, personal or public, who "volunteers" to die in order to end an epoch and to force us to confront the transitory nature of the world. Otherwise we just coast along, fat and happy, thinking we will live forever.

But this lesson must be continuously learned. By the time Emerson wrote "Compensation," having stepped off the path of convention he was treading in his twenties, he was becoming famous again as a writer, lecturer on the Lyceum circuit, and the most public face of "Transcendentalism." He had bought his capacious house in Concord, remarried, and had three children. Then on Jan. 27, 1842, his firstborn, five-year-old Waldo, died of scarlet fever, and again Emerson was plunged back into a kind of free-fall. "Sorrow make us all children again, destroys all differences of intellect. The wisest know nothing."9

At these times the loss seems to outweigh all that we still have--we cannot see past it. And when we fall into the personal and separate, it puts to the test our faith in and even knowledge of the Good. We see only injustice, privation, sorrow, calamity. Emerson certainly felt this too, as seen in his poem on Waldo's death, *Threnody*. It begins with a vivid account of his grief:

The South-wind brings Life, sunshine and desire,

And on every mount and meadow

Breathes aromatic fire;

But over the dead he has no power,

The lost, the lost, he cannot restore;

And, looking over the hills, I mourn

The darling who shall not return.

and goes on to describe Waldo's angelic nature. But just as he begins to lose himself in self-pity, "the deep Heart answered," and tells him:

But thou, my votary, weepest thou?

I gave thee sight--where is it now?

I taught thy heart beyond the reach

Of ritual, bible, or of speech; ...

Wilt thou not ope thy heart to know

What rainbows teach, and sunsets show?

Verdict which accumulates

From lengthening scroll of human fates,

Voice of earth to earth returned,

Prayers of saints that inly burned,--

Saying, *What is excellent,*

As God lives, is permanent;

Hearts are dust, hearts' loves remain;

Heart's love will meet thee again.

So although there is still the sense of separation, Emerson realizes that Waldo has not died, that there is always the Unity beyond the physical body. And some ten years later, he seems to address both the death of Ellen and Waldo in his poem *Brahma*, using a Sanskrit term for the One, acknowledging the Unity beyond the manifestations and dissolutions of our forms. We can know this Unity, but only if we let go of all our limitations, even the wish for immortality.

Brahma[9]

If the red slayer think he slays,

Or if the slain think he is slain,

They know not well the subtle ways

I keep, and pass, and turn again.

Far or forgot to me is near,

Shadow and sunlight are the same,

The vanished gods to me appear,

And one to me are shame and fame.

They reckon ill who leave me out;

When me they fly, I am the wings;

I am the doubter and the doubt,

And I the hymn the Brahmin sings.

The strong gods pine for my abode,

And pine in vain the sacred Seven;

But thou, meek lover of the good!

Find me, and turn thy back on heaven.

"That We Should Always Live in Perfect Holiness"-- *Plato, Meno*

As we've seen by now, knowledge of the Ideal as the form of the Good--eternal yet omnipresent, disembodied yet all-pervasive--leads naturally to a recognition of the immortality of our souls and those of all other "individuals" we see. In the passage in the Meno from which the above quote is taken, Socrates interrupts his inquiry into whether virtue can be taught and talks about what he has "heard from certain wise men and women who spoke of things divine,"

> And they say--mark now and see whether their words are true--they say that the soul of man is immortal, and at one time has an end, which is termed dying, and at another time is born again, but is never destroyed. And the moral is that a man ought to live always in perfect holiness. ...The soul then, as being immortal, and having been born again many times, and having seen all things that exist, whether in this world or in the world below, has knowledge of them all....

So Plato's formulation of immortality is not like the one found in most religions where you are born as a blank slate, live, and spend eternity in some place of reward or punishment based on your good or evil actions during your one life. It is more akin to the Eastern ideas of reincarnation, or eternal recurrence, where the soul goes "into" a body--maybe not even a human body--many times, but makes its own choice of body based on the experiences it has had in the previous one. He says that we are given guidance, we are given examples, but ultimately it is up to us whether we follow them, and choose the kind of life which will enable us to pursue unity with the One. In the Myth of Er in *The Republic* as well as other passages like the following from Phaedo, he makes it clear that we are in charge of our own destiny.

> But then, O my friends, he (Socrates) said, if the soul is really immortal, what care should be taken of her, not only in respect of the portion of time which is called life, but of eternity! And the danger of neglecting her from this point of view does indeed appear to be awful. If death had only been the end of all, the wicked would have had a good bargain in dying, for they would have been happily quit not only of their body, but of their own evil together with their souls. But now, inasmuch as the soul is manifestly immortal, there is no release or salvation from evil except the attainment of the highest virtue and wisdom.

Virtue! Wisdom! Holiness! I can see you now checking your watch to realize you have something else to do. This is of course the lament of the ego when faced with the prospect of having to change for the sake of attaining the bliss of the Good: you are trying to keep me from enjoying myself. Let's just keep this on a theoretical level where we can discuss indefinitely and I can go on doing whatever I want to do. That's what dialectic is about, right? Blah blah blah? Yadda yadda? After all, if it's all one, and it's only a play, then it doesn't really matter what I do, right?

Well, only if you're not planning to leave the play, whether through dying or through unifying, the first of which is inevitable and the second (if we believe our Idealists) desirable. So to paraphrase Socrates, the moral is that a man ought to live always in perfect readiness to be in the presence of the Good.[10]

And of course we always are in its presence, but don't usually realize it. Then there are those moments when the ego-shell falls away and we experience our own "infinitude." We are happy for no other reason than that it is our natural state to be happy; we have love and compassion for all other beings for no other reason than that they are expressions of the One. We lose all desires except the one that would have all beings feel this love and compassion. We realize that not only do we not have a right to those we love, we don't have a right to anything; that possession equals theft. We look with disbelief at the world of desire, anger, fear, division, and sorrow in which we spend most of our lives. Even its happinesses are small compared to that unconditional happiness. We feel we have come home, and wonder how we could ever leave.

Plotinus formulates it thus:

Anyone who has had this experience will know what I am talking about. He will know that the soul lives another life as it advances toward The One, reaches it and shares in it. Thus restored, the soul recognizes the presence of the dispenser of the true life. It needs nothing more. On the contrary, it must renounce everything else and rest in it alone, become it alone, all earthiness gone, eager to be free, impatient of every fetter that binds below in order so to embrace the real object of its love with its entire being that no part of it does not touch The One.[11]

And then he asks and answers the key question:

Why does a soul that has risen to the realm above not stay there? Because it has not yet entirely detached itself from the things here below.[12]

Detachment. One of the trickiest words in the spiritual vocabulary. The ego hears it and thinks "aloof, remote, above it all." But I believe it has more to do with this idea of ownership, of claiming rights to 1) our stuff and 2) our feelings about the stuff. We mistake the things we see as reality and we think if we can possess more things we will be more happy, in the way that some people want to possess great works of art or places of natural beauty. This is a sure sign of ego at work. Similarly, there is our attachment to a whole range of negative feelings engendered by this desire to possess. ("My preciousssss!") Most of us have no problem with viewing the Grand Canyon, feeling awestruck, and then walking away with no need to own it. But it's different with the things we do "possess;" my body, my house, my spouse, my children, my opinions, my religion. Detachment, though, would teach us to view them in the same way as the Canyon, with enjoyment, a sense of amazement, wonder, love, and humility. And the realization that we do not own any of them, and will have to give them up at some point whether we want to or not: there is no baggage check-in for Heaven (but by the same token, no security check either).

It's the same with those negative feelings that pull and push us away from the unified "presence;" anger, jealousy, resentment, envy, lust, greed, self-pity and self-aggrandizement. It is self-evident that these are totally incompatible with the state of happiness we are describing, but we allow them to run our lives anyway; we let people "make" us angry, we are jealous of another's good fortune, we are never satisfied with what we have but we fear we will lose it.

Pierre Hadot puts it this way, using the term "contemplation" for the state of unification:

How then should we live? For Plotinus, the great problem is to learn how to live our day-to-day life. We must learn to live, after contemplation, in such a way that we are once again prepared for contemplation. We must concentrate ourselves within, gathering ourselves together to the point that we can always be ready to receive the divine presence, when it manifests itself again. We must detach ourselves from life down here to such an extent that contemplation can become a continuous state. Nevertheless, we still have to learn how to put up with day-to-day life; better still, we must learn to illuminate it with the clear light that comes from contemplation.[13]

So just knowing about (*gnosis*) is not enough--we must also learn to live well, avoid duplicity, and bring our desires, thoughts and actions into harmony. As Plotinus says in Ennead II 9, *Against the Gnostics*:

> To say "look to God" is not helpful without some instruction as to what this looking imports: it might be very well said that one can "look" and still sacrifice no pleasure, still be the slave of impulse, repeating the word "God" but held in the grip of every passion and making no effort to master any. Virtue, advancing towards this Term and, linked together with thought, occupying a soul makes God manifest: "God" on the lips without a good conduct of life, is (only) a word.[14]

So a good first step is to become aware of these negative feelings when they present themselves, and just observe them instead of being swept away. Give up the idea that you are helpless before them; that your reaction, because it is automatic, is inevitable. See how they limit you and serve only the ego. Ask if this feeling perpetuates your illusion of limited selfhood. Ask if it is transitory, or permanent. Detach from these, says Plato, says Plotinus, says Ficino, and you will begin to "live in perfect holiness," practicing the art of dying. The gods, when we meet them, won't want to hear our complaints or see our resumés. They will only want to see how completely we have let go of anything that is not love.

1Plato, *Phaedo,* Benjamin Jowett, trans.

2Phaedo, the narrator of the dialogue, gives an accounting of those present, ending with the incongruous statement, "but Plato, if I am not mistaken, was ill."

3Eckhart Tolle, *Stillness Speaks,* New World Library 2003, p. 103

4The body is also closely aligned with the ego, which as we have seen, determines so many of the limited ideas we have about ourselves. The family into which our body is born can make us think we are a certain religion, nationality, or political persuasion. But the soul knows it is none of these.

5Marsilio Ficino, *The Platonic Theology*, Michael J.B. Allen, trans., Harvard University Press, I Tatti Renaissance Library, 2001

6Michael J.B. Allen, trans., op. cit

7In *The Over-Soul,* he makes the same point:

> Men ask concerning the immortality of the soul, the employments of heaven, the state of the sinner, and so forth. They even dream that Jesus has left replies to precisely these interrogatories. Never a moment did that sublime spirit speak in their patois. To truth, justice, love, the attributes of the soul, the idea of immutableness is essentially associated. Jesus, living in these moral sentiments, heedless of sensual fortunes, heeding only the manifestations of these, never made the separation of the idea of duration from

the essence of these attributes, nor uttered a syllable concerning the duration of the soul. It was left to his disciples to sever duration from the moral elements, and to teach the immortality of the soul as a doctrine, and maintain it by evidences. The moment the doctrine of the immortality is separately taught, man is already fallen. In the flowing of love, in the adoration of humility, there is no question of continuance. No inspired man ever asks this question, or condescends to these evidences. For the soul is true to itself, and the man in whom it is shed abroad cannot wander from the present, which is infinite, to a future which would be finite.

[8]Ralph Waldo Emerson, *Emerson in His Journals,* selected and edited by Joel Porte, Harvard University Press, 1982, p. 74-75

[9]The reference to the "red slayer" has been seen as a symbol for the blood from Ellen's tuberculosis as well as the scarlet fever that took Waldo. The third verse is quoted in W. Somerset Maugham's *The Razor's Edge.*

[10]"...we ought to fly away from the earth to heaven as quickly as we can; and to fly away is to become like God, as far as this is possible: and to become like him, is to become holy, just, and wise. But, O my friend, you cannot easily convince mankind that they should pursue virtue or avoid vice, not merely in order that man may seem to be good, which is the reason given by the world, and in my judgment is only a repetition of an old wives' fable. Whereas, the truth is that God is never in any way unrighteous--he is perfect

righteousness, and he of us who is the most righteous is most like him." Plato, *Theaetetus*

[11]Plotinus, *The Essential Plotinus,* translation by Elmer O'Brien, S. J., 1964, Hackett Publishing, p. 86

[12]Plotinus, op. cit. MacKenna's translation (Penguin, 1991) is more forceful: "escaped."

[13]Pierre Hadot, *Plotinus, or the Simplicity of Vision*, Michael Chase, trans., University of Chicago, 1993

[14]Plotinus,*The Enneads,* translated by Stephen MacKenna, Penguin, 1993, p. 127 Parenthesis mine. I might also say that I find the opposite problem with the Stoics (Epictetus, Marcus Aurelius, etc.): they teach us to bear hardships and make sacrifices, but without acknowledging that we do so to discover the Ideal within us.

Chapter XVI: The Hero's Quest

As I stated in the episode on Shakespeare, many of our most enduring stories can be seen as allegories for the loss and attempted recovery of our relationship with The One. In many of Shakespeare's king plays, the rightful king is deposed, assassinated or unwisely abdicates, leaving the kingdom open to the workings of the ego: duality, conflict, ambition, desire and murder, to name a few. Of course this story-form did not originate with Shakespeare; these themes exist from the earliest known stories and myths of nearly all cultures. When seen in this light, the question of whether the events "actually happened" becomes moot; they are always happening, within each of us. In this chapter we will look at a representative story from the Greek tradition, that of Minos, Theseus, and the Minotaur.

The use of myth is another way people have invented to speak about the indescribable. That we are separated from the Good—our exile from Eden, our drinking of the waters of Lethe—which is our true immortal nature, is the fundamental fact of our existence as humans, and our attempt to reunite with it is the fundamental work we do. Descriptions of how we do this work constitute the bulk of our myths. Some, like the Iliad, have to do with our attempts to reclaim something of beauty (Helen), which has been stolen from us (by our "resident thief"), or in another allegory, our attempts to return to our home and rightful union, like Odysseus single-mindedly seeking Ithaca and Penelope, despite the temptations and obstacles along the way.

One of the most prevalent genres of myth is the "test and quest," decoded most thoroughly by the poet of mythology Joseph Campbell. As a reminder, in his classic work *The Hero with a Thousand Faces*,[1] he calls this the monomyth.

> A hero ventures forth from the world of common day into a region of supernatural wonder: fabulous forces are there encountered and a decisive victory is won: the hero comes back from this mysterious adventure with the power to bestow boons on his fellow man.

Although much of Campbell's work draws on non-Western myths, the principles and quest elements he describes still apply. They can all be seen as allegories for the process whereby the individual overcomes his own multiplicity to realize The One. They are not always as clear-cut as we might like, but if they weren't, we would probably never look beyond their entertaining outer surface.

> Minos was the son of Zeus and Europa. In keeping with his illustrious ancestry, he seemed destined to assume sovereignty over Crete from his base at Knossos. However, one day his claim to power was contested; so he prayed to Poseidon to send confirmation of his right to rule, in the form of a bull from the sea[2], which he would reciprocate by sacrificing. Poseidon sent the bull, but Minos broke his side of the bargain, keeping the special bull and sacrificing an ordinary one instead. Poseidon's reaction was to instill into Minos' wife Pasiphae an unnatural lust for the bull. To fulfill her desires she climbed into an artificial cow prefabricated by Daidalos, Minos' resident technological genius. The two mated,

and the strange fruit of their union was the Minotaur: bull-faced, human-bodied and carnivorous. Minos shut it away in another of Daidalos' inventions: the maze known as the Labyrinth.[3]

So although Pasiphae's lust gave birth to the Minotaur, the original sin was that of Minos by keeping the god-sent bull for himself, his own lust to possess. As Campbell says:

> He had converted a public event into personal gain, whereas the whole sense of his investiture as king had been that he was no longer a mere private person. The return of the bull should have symbolized his absolutely selfless submission to the functions of his role. The retaining of it represented, on the other hand, an impulse to egocentric self-aggrandizement. ...By the sacrilege of the refusal of the rite, however, the individual cut himself as a unit off from the larger unit of the whole community: and so the One was broken into the many, and these then battled each other—each out for himself—and could be governed only by force.

The Minotaur—the half-man, the monster, the dragon—takes up residence. So our own "king," when it becomes an ego, or abdicates to an ego, depending on how you look at it, causes the same kind of disintegration. What is by nature a coherent whole becomes split into separate senses, a mind, a heart, a will, a body, all at war with each other, but with the memory of a "golden age" when they were One. There comes a labyrinth where there had been a straight line.

Once the disintegration is set in motion, it becomes self-perpetuating. In order to feed the Minotaur, Minos requires the people of Athens to send each year fourteen young people to serve as food for the carnivorous beast; the best is consumed by the worst. In this arrangement, the king of Athens, Aigeus, is also culpable for agreeing to it, even though it was brought on through coercion.

Enter the hero of the story, Theseus, the son of Aigeus, the rightful heir whose existence was unknown to him.4 To return to Buxton's description of what happens next:

> Minos had not reckoned with Theseus' valour, nor with the capacity of the females of the Cretan royal line (including Europa, Pasiphae, and Phaidra) to yearn for the attractions of a stranger—or of the strange. When Theseus valiantly volunteered to join the next party of youths destined to be the Minotaur's tributary meal, what saved him was the love of Minos' daughter Ariadne. On Daidalos' advice she told Theseus to unwind a thread attached to the entrance of the maze, so as to be able to retrace his steps once he had killed the Minotaur.

Theseus is successful, runs off with Ariadne, but whom, in an apparent state of forgetfulness, he leaves behind on the island of Naxos.5 Another bout of forgetfulness by Theseus causes Aigeus to commit suicide, and so when he lands, Theseus is made the new king of Athens.

Without being overly simplistic, we can see here that when the old king becomes compromised, a new one must arise in the form of an inner hero who is willing to take on the risks of descending into the labyrinth (or the cave, or the underworld) that is home to the ego-monster, and killing it. (If you're a pacifist, that may sound harsh, but you can't negotiate or compromise with the ego.) One escapes from the labyrinth through a combination of love (Ariadne) and knowledge (Daidalos).[6] For us, the quest is not nearly so dangerous, although just as rewarding.

Campbell again:

> The flax for the linen of his thread he has gathered from the fields of the human imagination. Centuries of husbandry, decades of diligent culling, the work of numerous hearts and hands, have gone into the hackling, sorting, and spinning of this tightly twisted yarn. Furthermore, we have not even to risk the adventure alone; for the heroes of all time have gone before us; the labyrinth is thoroughly known; we have only to follow the thread of the hero-path. And where we had thought to find an abomination, we shall find a god; where we had thought to slay another, we shall slay ourselves, where we had thought to travel outward, we shall come to the center of our own existence; where we had thought to *be alone, we shall be with the whole world.*

But in myth, the monster never really dies, so the new king is always subject to his own fall. Le roi est mort. Vive le roi. And the story goes on.

The Cave as Hero's Quest

Socrates, as portrayed by Plato, had a rather ambivalent view of mythology, unless we can ascribe his attitudes to Socratic irony. While he was clearly familiar with his Hesiod and Homer and gods and heroes, he makes a point in *The Republic* of saying that the ideal state would bar the telling of most myths on the grounds that the stories of bad behavior among the gods would be a corrupting influence on the children. (Rather like parents feel about comic books.) He specifically mentions the story about the uncertain parentage of Theseus to which I alluded in the last section:

> And let us equally refuse to believe, or allow to be repeated, the tale of Theseus son of Poseidon, or of Peirithous son of Zeus, going forth as they did to perpetrate a horrid rape; or of any other hero or son of a god daring to do such impious and dreadful things as they falsely ascribe to them in our day: and let us further compel the poets to declare either that these acts were not done by them, or that they were not the sons of gods; – both in the same breath they shall not be permitted to affirm. We will not have them trying to persuade our youth that the gods are the authors of evil, and that heroes are no better than men–sentiments which, as we were saying, are neither pious nor true, for we have already proved that evil cannot come from the gods.7

Socrates himself is evidence of the fact that hearing these stories need not inflict damage on young souls, and he also clearly recognizes the power and value of stories in communicating philosophical points. In this and the next episode I'd like to look at a couple of instances in the Republic where he uses the form of the "test and quest" myth to make some key points.

The first of these is the allegory of the Cave in Book 7, which was discussed in Chapter IV, but it is so simple and so rich at the same time, that I think it's worth another visit. As you may recall, Plato creates an image of prisoners in a cave since birth who can look only at shadows which are projected by a fire onto a wall in front of them.[8] (*Glaucon: You have shown me a strange image, and they are strange prisoners. Socrates: Like ourselves, I replied....*) Since they have no other frame of reference, they take these shadows to be reality: "To them, I said, the truth would be literally nothing but the shadows of these images." It is necessary to remember that in this analogy, the shadows are the things we see and the thoughts we think.

Now although none of the prisoners "hears the call" or is inspired to break free of his chains by himself, Plato does speculate on what would happen if they "are released and disabused of their error." In the first scenario, a prisoner is forced to turn around and look into the light of the fire and ultimately "forced into the presence of the sun himself." Since he has not been prepared for this ascent from the cave, "his eyes will be dazzled, and he will not be able to see anything at all of what are now called realities." This is a good description of what can happen when people try to expand consciousness through the continued use of drugs.

In the other scenario however, the prisoner is led through the ascent presumably by guides who have made the journey themselves. He first sees the fire and the objects passing in front of it, and realizes that what he thought to be real was just an illusion. Then he is shown "the reflections of men and other objects in the water, and then the objects themselves," gradually increasing his ability to see until he is shown the sun itself, the child of the Good, "in his own proper place, and not in another; and he will contemplate him as he is." Then from seeing, he will be led to reason that the sun is "the guardian of all that is in the visible world, and in a certain way the cause of all the things which he and his fellows have been accustomed to behold."

This, for Plato, is the "land of supernatural wonder," and learning to reason, to exist in the intelligible realm, is the "decisive victory." Since the former prisoner now sees the reality of what he formerly believed to be true, he can have compassion for the prisoners still in the cave: "Would he not say with Homer, 'better to be the poor servant of a poor master,' and to endure anything, rather than think as they do and live after their manner?"

But while Plato does believe in the necessity of the hero's return, he is only too aware of the risks that are posed by bestowing boons on those still staring at shadows: he in fact had the example of Socrates. "Men would say of him that up he went and down he came without his eyes; and that it was better not even to think of ascending; and if any one tried to loose another and lead him up to the light, let them only catch the offender, and they would put him to death."

So the newly enlightened one, who has seen "the universal author of all things beautiful and right," runs the risk, like Socrates, like Jesus, of being killed by those whom they tried to free.

Plato also realizes that "those who attain this beatific vision are unwilling to descend into human affairs; for their souls are ever hastening into the upper world where they desire to dwell...." But he believes it is the duty of the enlightened ones to make the return to the cave and become the philosopher-kings, since only they can administer the state with justice, and their very reluctance to govern is their main qualification for it.

> Whereas the truth is that the State in which the rulers are most reluctant to govern is always the best and most quietly governed, and the State in which they are most eager, the worst.
> Quite true, he replied
> And will our pupils, when the hear this, refuse to take their turn at the toils of the State, when they are allowed to spend the greater part of their time with one another in the heavenly light?
> So because they have "seen the beautiful and just and good in their truth," they can return to their state of enlightenment even while serving as kings.

Now without wishing to belabor the obvious, I would like to make the point that this quest is also the one that we must make as individuals to realize the Good within ourselves. All along, of course, Plato has been using the larger State as an analogy for the individual one.[9] Most discussions of the Republic focus on the larger State since looking at ourselves is

235

the kind of uncomfortable examination we try to avoid at all costs. But I think Plato is really talking about our own inner government: how we free the soul from the illusions of the ego and return the philosopher to his rightful kingship.

The ego is our "common day," our usual state in which we take the things we see and the thoughts we think to be true, even though they are obviously transient, always becoming, never being. But when something awakens the soul, our connection to the eternal–and unfortunately this often comes in the form of a tragedy or other hardship–it can see the futility of living a life amidst ephemera, and start to make this upward journey in search of the Ideal. At each step of the way we will meet with resistance from the ego, which is quite happy in its world of illusion. But when we do realize our own inner philosopher-king–we trade facts for Truth, thinking for Consciousness, pleasure for Bliss–our "decisive victory" is won. We have penetrated to the heart of the labyrinth and killed the Minotaur. While there is always the chance of being killed by the ego on our return, we now have the possibility of governing it, transforming it into a persona, a "mask" through which we can see the world and the infinite variety and drama of the Ideal, while still spending "the greater part of (our) time with one another in the heavenly light."

The Myth of Er

At the end of *The Republic,* Plato again uses a hero quest form to make points about the immortality

of the soul, and the need for the philosopher to live always in virtue and justice. As he says also in *Meno,*
And they say—mark now and see whether their words are true—they say that the soul of man is immortal, and at one time has an end, which is termed dying, and at another time is born again, but is never destroyed. And the moral is that a man ought to live always in perfect holiness."

To support this assertion, Plato tells the story of "a hero, Er the son of Armenius, a Pamphylian by birth."[10] He had been killed in a battle, and when the bodies were collected some ten days later (ugh!), his was found to be in a state of preservation, "unaffected by decay." Nonetheless, two days later it was placed on a funeral pyre to be burned, but "he returned to life and told them what he had seen in the other world."

He said that when his soul left the body he went on a journey with a great company, and that they came to a mysterious place at which there were two openings in the earth; they were near together, and over against them were two other openings in the heaven above. In the intermediate space there were judges seated, who commanded the just, after they had given judgment on them and had bound their sentences in front of them, to ascend by the heavenly way on the right hand; and in like manner the unjust were bidden by them to descend by the lower way on the left hand; these also bore the symbols of their deeds, but fastened on their backs. He drew near, and they told him that he was to be the messenger who would carry the report of the other world to men, and they bade him hear and see all that was to be heard and seen in that place. Then he beheld and saw on one side the souls departing at either opening of heaven and earth when sentence had been given on them; and at the two other openings other souls, some ascending out of the earth dusty and worn with travel, some descending out of heaven clean and bright. And arriving ever and anon they seemed to have come from a long journey, and they went forth with gladness into the meadow, where they encamped as at a festival; and those who knew one another embraced and conversed, the souls which came from earth curiously enquiring about the things above, and the souls which came from heaven about the things beneath. And they told one another of what had happened by the way, those from below weeping and sorrowing at the remembrance of the things which they had endured and seen in their journey beneath the earth (now the journey lasted a thousand years), while those from above were describing heavenly delights and visions of inconceivable beauty. The story, Glaucon, would take too long to tell; but the sum was this: —He said that for every wrong which they had done to any one they suffered tenfold; or once in a hundred years —such being reckoned to be the length of man's life, and the penalty being thus paid ten times in a thousand years. If, for example, there were any who had been the cause of many deaths, or had betrayed or enslaved cities or armies, or been guilty of any other evil behaviour, for each and all of their offences they received punishment ten times over, and the rewards of beneficence and justice and holiness were in the same proportion.

Plato goes on to describe some of the punishments, especially those of tyrants, in rather vivid detail. I've previously compared this recounting with the traditional judgment stories of Christianity and their depictions in art. A key difference is that in Christian doctrine, humans have one life and are assigned forever to heaven or hell (or purgatory) based on their actions in it. Plato goes on to describe a system of reincarnation in which the souls choose their own lives and destinies.[11]

A prophet or interpreter of the Fate Lachesis addresses the assembled souls and says, "Hear the word of Lachesis, the daughter of Necessity. Mortal souls, behold a new cycle of life and mortality. Your genius[12] will not be allotted to you, but you choose your genius; and let him who draws the first lot have the first choice, and the life which he chooses shall be his destiny. Virtue is free, and as a man honours or dishonours her he will have more or less of her; the responsibility is with the chooser –God is justified." So again, we are responsible for making our own choice of life, but from Er's description, we don't seem any more likely to choose well before we are born than we do after. "Most curious, he said, was the spectacle –sad and laughable and strange; for the choice of the souls was in most cases based on their experience of a previous life."

Of course one may well ask if we can see the course and circumstances of our lives before we live them, why would anyone choose a life of hardship and limitation as so many seem to do? Well, for Plato, our lives are not about being enjoyed for their own sake: they are opportunities to learn the distinction between the evil of selfishness and the limitless Good, and only knowledge of the Good can bring permanent happiness.

And here, my dear Glaucon, is the supreme peril of our human state; and therefore the utmost care should be taken. Let each one of us leave every other kind of knowledge and seek and follow one thing only, if peradventure he may be able to learn and may find someone who will make him able to learn and discern between good and evil, and so to choose always and everywhere the better life as he has opportunity. He should consider the bearing of all these things which have been mentioned severally and collectively upon virtue; he should know what the effect of beauty is when combined with poverty or wealth in a particular soul, and what are the good and evil consequences of noble and humble birth, of private and public station, of strength and weakness, of cleverness and dullness, and of all the soul, and the operation of them when conjoined; he will then look at the nature of the soul, and from the consideration of all these qualities he will be able to determine which is the better and which is the worse; and so he will choose, giving the name of evil to the life which will make his soul more unjust, and good to the life which will make his soul more just; all else he will disregard. For we have seen and know that this is the best choice both in life and after death. A man must take with him into the world below an adamantine faith in truth and right, that there too he may be undazzled by the desire of wealth or the other allurements of evil, lest, coming upon tyrannies and similar villainies, he do irremediable wrongs to others and suffer yet worse himself; but let him know how to choose the mean and avoid the extremes on either side, as far as possible, not only in this life but in all that which is to come. For this is the way of happiness.

So after the souls have chosen they are tied to their new lives and genii by the Fates and sent off through the plain of Forgetfulness and to drink the water of the river of Unmindfulness, "and those that were not saved by wisdom drank more than was necessary; and as each one as he drank forgot all things."

Each one except Er, who completes his hero's quest by returning to life and giving mankind this boon of his knowledge. We do not choose our lives in this afterworld once every thousand years; we choose them at each moment. The reality of The Good is available to us at each moment. So now you know.

And thus, Glaucon, the tale has been saved and has not perished, and will save us if we are obedient to the word spoken; and we shall pass safely over the river of Forgetfulness and our soul will not be defiled. Wherefore my counsel is that we hold fast ever to the heavenly way and follow after justice and virtue always, considering that the soul is immortal and able to endure every sort of good and every sort of evil. Thus shall we live dear to one another and to the gods, both while remaining here and when, like conquerors in the games who go round to gather gifts, we receive our reward. And it shall be well with us both in this life and in the pilgrimage of a thousand years which we have been describing.

[1]Joseph Campbell, *The Hero with a Thousand Faces,* Princeton, 1968

[2]Minos was the son of Zeus, the supreme god, but was conceived when Zeus took the form of a bull and mated with Europa; the bull was therefore emblematic of Minos.

[3]Richard Buxton, *The Complete World of Greek Mythology,* Thames and Hudson, 2004

[4]I won't get into the whole back story here, but Theseus could possibly also claim the god Poseidon as his father, helpful in being a hero. You could look it up.

[5]Unfortunate, perhaps, but she does eventually marry a god, Dionysos, and get her own opera (*Ariadne auf Naxos,* by Richard Strauss).

[6]After this defining episode, Theseus goes on to have a rich mythical afterlife, including an improbable marriage to another of Minos' daughters, Phaidra.

[7]Plato, *The Republic*, Book 3

[8]As is frequently pointed out, a more current, not necessarily better, analogy is that of a movie theater, or any of the proliferating number of screens at which we spend our day staring, especially when they are showing oxymoronic "reality television."

[9]Plato, *The Republic*, Book 2.

> I will tell you, I replied; justice, which is the subject of our enquiry, is, as you know, sometimes spoken of as the virtue of an

individual, and sometimes as a virtue of the State. True, he replied.

And is not a State larger than an individual?

It is.

Then in the larger the quantity of justice is likely to be larger and more easily discernible. I propose therefore that we enquire into the nature of justice and injustice, first as they appear in the State, and secondly in the individual, proceeding from the greater to the lesser and comparing them.

That, he said, is an excellent proposal.

10Pamphylia is a region in southern modern Turkey, whose name in Greek, Παμφυλία, means "of mingled tribes or races." This story does not appear anywhere else in Greek mythology, so it is possible that Plato made it up.

11Before this though, Plato interjects an extended passage describing "the Spindle of Necessity," a representation of the solar system in which there are eight concentric orbiting shafts of different colors rotating in different directions. I will admit that the significance of this description eludes me, except insofar as Plato says that "the eight together form one harmony," and imply an orderly and lawful method for the events that follow.

12This is "genius" in the original sense of "something born with," which Plato later describes as ""the guardian of their lives and the fulfiller of the choice...." This idea persisted through millennia of Western culture–Emerson speaks of Wordsworth's obeying "the inward promptings of his heavenly genius," (The

Natural History of the Intellect) but he also refers to it in the past tense: "The ancients believed that a genius or demon took possession at birth of each mortal, to guide him; that these genii were sometimes seen as a flame of fire partly immersed in the bodies which they governed; — on an evil man, resting on his head; in a good man, mixed with his substance." (The Conduct of Life–Beauty). Few today have the older sense of it--we seem to mistake "everyone has a genius" for "everyone is a genius."

Epilogue: The Ideal in the Planet

Although the Ideal, as we have been studying it is a product of Western thought, it is universal in its reach and can bestow its beauty and happiness on peoples everywhere. It does not encourage division into the narrower and narrower categories by which we define ourselves, but makes us aware of our common humanity at each moment. In an age where we are becoming simultaneously more connected and more isolated, this is an important lesson to learn. We need to see past the visible, the surface differences, to the universal souls within, but also require that these individual souls not limit themselves by these differences. Do not confuse your name with the reality of yourself, and do not confuse the names of the Good with the reality of Itself.

There is within each of us a universe as limitless and rich as the physical universe. But as with that universe, we tend to stay close to home, living with our dragons, because it is familiar. If we can learn to become still, to distinguish between the Real and the shadows, the eternal and the transient, between ideas and the Idea, all limitations will fall away and we realize that the Ideal has always been there.

We are all in Love in the same way that we are all in air. Don't forget to breathe.

NOTE FROM THE AUTHOR

I claim copyright to this work with some reservations, since I feel that "intellectual property" is an oxymoron. No one "owns" the words; no one "owns" the ideas. This kind of work should probably be done anonymously, with no claims. But one does have a stewardship responsibility over the expression of ideas, and also those who do this kind of work need food, shelter, and *otium cum dignitate*. (You could look it up.) Therefore, feel free to quote this work, but be sure to include proper references.

Index of Philosophers

Anaxagoras, 17-19, 24, 29, 33, 35

Anaximander, 9-10

Emerson, Ralph Waldo, 5, 93, 115, 137, 138, 141-153, 157-160, 165, 166, 171-177, 191, 195, 196, 200, 211, 213-215

Empedocles, 15-18

Ficino, Marsilio, 98, 100-102, 106, 109-112, 116, 121, 125, 129, 134-136, 151, 169, 193, 203, 210, 212

Heraclitus, 15, 21, 124

Melissus of Samos, 10-11

Parmenides, 12-14, 62, 68

Pico (della Mirandola), 100, 102, 104, 106, 121

Plato, 5, 6, 12, 16, 17, 26, 29, 31-37, 39, 45, 50-52, 57-59, 61, 64-70, 73, 77, 79, 89-99, 102, 104-108, 111-112, 116, 117, 120, 124, 125, 128, 129, 130, 133, 136, 137, 138, 147, 158, 159, 164, 168, 180, 194, 195, 199, 201-203, 207-212, 218, 219, 223, 232-239

Plotinus, 72-86, 88-90, 95, 104, 106, 111, 119, 124, 125, 129, 169, 195, 203, 204, 210, 212, 220-223

Socrates, 6, 10, 12, 19, 26, 29, 31-37, 39-56, 60-67, 73, 75, 124, 147, 163, 167, 168, 173, 202, 208, 209, 212-213, 218-220, 232-235

Taylor, Thomas, 136-138, 145, 212

Thales, 7-9

Xenophanes, 11-12

23233667R00154

Made in the USA
Charleston, SC
16 October 2013